ENERGY USE IN AGRICULTURAL PRODUCTIVITY

About the Author

Hifzur Rehman is Senior Reader in Geography at the Aligarh Muslim University, Aligarh. Dr. Rehman has an extensive experience in teaching at the undergraduate and postgraduate levels. He has an unparallel ability in simplifying difficult concepts in the subject and to analyse enormous facts in a cogent manner. His major fields of interest are Agricultural Geography, Resource Geography and Physical Geography.

ENERGY USE
IN
AGRICULTRAL PRODUCTIVITY

HIFZUR REHMAN
Department of Geography
Aligarh Muslim University
Aligarh

CONCEPT PUBLISHING COMPANY, NEW DELHI-110059

ISBN 81-8069-077-6

First Published 2003

Published and Printed by
Ashok Kumar Mittal
Concept Publishing Company
A/15-16, Commercial Block, Mohan Garden
New Delhi-110059 (INDIA)
Phones : 25351460, 25351794
Fax : 091-11-25357103
Email : publishing@conceptpub.com.

Foreword

India's population in 2003 stands at 1.07 billion and the projected population in 2025 is 1.35 billion. The foodgrains production in 1999-2000 was about 209 million tonnes and by 2025 the requirement at the current rate of consumption, which is inadequate, would be 250 million tonnes. It would largely depend on the increased application of energy through chemicalization, bio-fertilizers, organic manures and consequently enhanced agricultural productivity. Agricultural productivity depends partly on the fertility of soil and partly on the efficiency of the farmers, the availability of irrigation, the use of implements and the management of the systems of land use. Various methods have been applied to measure the agricultural productivity and agricultural efficiency.

In case of agricultural efficiency, higher the productivity of foodgrains, higher is the efficiency of the farmer. But it would be appropriate to consider the input-output ratio. Countries where the input is higher, the yield per hectare is high. While in case of India the average yield of foodgrains is one of the lowest in the world. The New Agricultural Technology has helped the country in increasing the yield per hectare, but it is still much lower compared to the advanced countries of the world, particularly the West European countries.

Dr. Hifzur Rehman has not only discussed the concept of energy use in agriculture but has thoroughly examined the measurements of energy efficiency and methods of measurements of agricultural productivity, and makes a comparison of the use of energy in the developed and developing countries.

The study has been meticulously done and arrives at the conclusion that in judging the efficiency of Indian farmer, energy use must be taken into consideration.

It is a work of great importance in agricultural geography and shall be useful to all those interested in the studies of agricultural productivity and agricultural efficiency. It is an innovative study in land use.

Mohammad Shafi
Professor Emeritus
Department of Geography
Aligarh Muslim University
Aligarh-202002, India

Preface

Agricultural practices in developing countries of the world have changed with the advent of "green revolution" since the mid-1960s' when the high-yielding varieties of seeds for wheat from Mexico and for rice from Philippines were brought and introduced in respective cropping areas of the country. These genetically improved varieties of wheat and rice, and some other crops required more irrigation, fertilizers, fuels, and insecticides. Therefore, all the improved practices for these crops together with energy inputs applied in production have to be evaluated while ascertaining their impact on the levels of food production and productivity.

The aim of this book is to take into account some of the aspects of energy use in agriculture and provide some explanations with regard to agricultural efficiency and crop productivity.

The entire work has been divided into five chapters. Chapter 1 deals with the energy use in agriculture and highlights the meaning and concepts of energy use. In Chapter 2 an attempt has been made to give a comprehensive assessment to review the existing literature with regard to the measurement of energy efficiency in food production systems of developed and developing countries. Chapter 3 deals with the concepts of agricultural efficiency and crop productivity together with some methods of its measurements. A comparative assessment of energy use in farming systems of some selected crops and countries belonging to developed and developing countries is presented in Chapter 4. Some results pertaining to energy use in farming and a few surveys conducted in some selected villages belonging to some Development Blocks of six Tehsils of district Aligarh are presented in Chapter 5.

I acknowledge with gratitude the help which I have received from Professor Mohammad Shafi (Professor Emeritus) in the preparation of this book. My thanks are also due to Professor Azimuddin Qureshi, Chairman, Department of Geography, Aligarh Muslim University, Aligarh for providing all the facilities in the Department to complete the work. Mr. Mukammil Husain, Research Scholar in the Department of Geography has been of much help all the times for making necessary corrections in the typed matter. I am much indebted for his kind assistance I received in this regard. My thanks are also due to Mr. H.K. Sharma for typing the manuscript on computer within a limited time besides his professional interests and many preoccupations.

Hifzur Rehman

Contents

List of Tables

List of Figures

Introdcution

The major problems in the process of economic development requiring immediate action is : self-sufficiency in foodgrains and energy requirements. The strategies recommended at the World Food Conference held at Rome, November 5-16, 1974 under the auspices of the United Nations relied heavily on the application of more energy in crop production – in terms of irrigation, fertilizers, machines and pesticides. Emphasis was laid on the adoption of North American type of highly – intensive agriculture to increase the yield of crops in the developing countries. Agricultural practices in many of the developing countries have become energy-intensive. More recently serious concern has been voiced whether such a strategy is desirable in an age of 'energy crisis', when many of the developing countries including India are facing serious balance of payment problem.

It appears that it may not be possible to adopt the systems prevalent in developed countries to increase our agricultural production. With the latest strategies incorporated in agriculture, the 'green revolution' type of high-yielding varieties were introduced in India. The new strains of cereals, pulses, oilseeds, sugarcane, and potatoes need more fertilizers, pesticides and irrigation to yield more, but development should not be at the cost of environment. It is therefore, important that, while increasing the irrigation facilities, drainage should be improved so that waterlogging may not occur. Similarly with the use of chemicalization bio-fertilizer, blue-green algae, green manures and organic manures may also be used to improve the structure of soil.

In order to examine the judicious use of energy resources, it was attempted to evaluate various aspects of crop cultivation and production in Aligarh district. The entire crop production systems have been evaluated in Aligarh in relation to energy requirements.

The basic objective of the study is to ascertain the use of energy and its efficiency in crop production system.

As the cultivation of crop follows a sequence of a number of agronomic practices, the mode of energy use varies from traditional methods of crop cultivation to transitional, and from transitional to modern. By examining the relationship between the energy inputs and the relative yield of crops obtained, it is easy to identify the relative importance of each of energy input and to evaluate the potential for energy conservation.

1

The Concept of Energy Use in Agriculture

A. ENERGY USE IN AGRICULTURE

Crop cultivation is the human activity on the earth's surface that transforms solar energy into useful (edible) chemical energy by means of plants and animals. Plants receive a major portion of energy from the sun, and that energy is converted into chemical by photosynthesis in green plants (autotrophs), a process by which carbon dioxide and water are converted to sugar within plant cells that contain chlorophyll. The total amount of solar energy thus converted into chemical energy is called 'gross primary energy'. This energy stored within the plant is used for the maintenance of different tissues and sustain the growth, and a part of that energy is preserved by the seed for propagation. The energy utilized through the metabolic process within the living organism is described as the 'somatic energy' (Newcombe, 1976).

Different plants utilize solar energy in a number of ways to transform carbon dioxide, soil nutrients, water into plant tissues, sugars, and other materials that are used either directly or indirectly for food. Different forms of energy that have been incorporated by man into agriculture are referred to as 'cultural energy' and the inputs forming it can be grouped as biological and industrial areas. Human and animal labour are the two most obvious forms of biological inputs, but the addition of organic matter, such as animal manure is not incorporated with these two, and has a class of its own. Industrial energy inputs are those derived by means of modern technologies of electric power devices used in agricultural production, from fossil fuels, or from sources such as radioactive materials, geothermal sources, or flowing water. Some sources of industrial energy, such as fossil fuels are non-renewable, others such as hydroelectric energy is renewable.

Energy inputs to agricultural activities are both immediate and indirect. A farmer ploughing with a tractor for example, is expending energy both in human labour and through fuel consumption. However, he is also utilizing a device, the tractor, that requires land and varied expenditures of energy to produce.

Cultural energy inputs applied in crop production in the form of fertilizers, water, pesticides and management of cultivation are significantly capable of enhancing the trapping of solar energy within the period of crop maturity. That is referred to as the 'extra somatic energy', which flows through or is utilized by a human community through metabolic process within a living organism (Newcombe, 1976). The efficiency of both solar and cultural energy in their utilization and the relative cost benefit relationship of different forms of cultural energy used in a specific farming system determines the efficiency and cost-competitiveness of that system.

Until recently, crop production has been assessed by taking into consideration the time span, space dimension and in terms of money the inputs invested and the output derived. However, the recent awareness about the energy needs of technology has led to a critical assessment of the energy input-output relationships in crop production. The entire food system involves an assessment of 'on production technology' and 'post-harvest technology'. A large number of operations are needed by an individual crop until it is harvested and before leaving the farmgate to reach the consumer. These operations encompass the two phases of activities – the pre-harvest and post-harvest, and in a separate order ranging from tilling of land to the final distribution and consumption of crop output. These activities are followed in different forms and orders for different crops, and the mode of operations vary in accordance with the nature of work, income levels of the farmers, location of field, and so on.

The input to agriculture i.e., the 'support energy' or 'energy subsidy' (energy other than that derived directly from solar radiation), as it is called include all the items involving an expenditure of energy from expendable resources. Its intensity refers to gross energy requirement per unit area. The amount of solar energy is not included in this counting because it is available in abundant form and distributed uniformly over larger areas. The energy output of the production of crop is generally the metabolisable energy obtained from the food. Apart from the items of output consumable by man as food, there are certain other products, such as crop residues, animal wastes and manure, all of which have a use to man either directly or indirectly by re-cycling through the crop-animal chain. However, these by-products are not included, not because they are less important, but because of that the prime purpose of agriculture is the production of food.

Depending on the purpose and nature of use, the input committed to agriculture include both direct and indirect consumption of material resources. Where direct input refers to the energy resource that is consumed on the farm and which is depeleted within a short period, such as chemical fertilizers, seeds and chemicals, and the indirect input refers to energy consumed some where off the form to manufacture durable inputs such as modern agricultural implements and farm machinery. The energy requirement in agriculture for crop sustenance depend upon different inputs in the form of traction power, seeds, fertilizers, irrigation and plant protection chemicals besides human and animal power which in turn are expressed in terms of primary energy equivalences. Various inputs consumed by agriculture can be transformed into common energy measure based on caloric value by combustion. But the energy contained in seeds and the total output is expressed in nutritive (alimentary) calories. As a primary source of energy solar radiation through photosynthesis in crop cultivation generates alimentary calories, whereas the fossil-fuels based inputs utilized for the generation of calories aim to put the plant in best condition and to increase the mobilization of solar energy. For animals, metabolic calories be considered by measuring the protein, vitamin or amino acid content.

On the basis of cultivation technologies incorporated, the

agricultural practices may be the primitive (or traditional), improved (or transitional) and modern. In primitive or traditional agricultural systems, the process of crop cultivation involves no change in indigenous practices and that are carried virtually in their natural state, that is the principal source of energy is sun which is slightly augmented by human and animal energy, with well irrigation, use of local varieties of seeds and a complete dependence upon traditional sources of manuring. The only commercial energy input in traditional farming is that required to produce hand tools and animal implements. Since the traditional farms use no commercial fertilizer and the plants seeds are retained from previous crop, there is no commercial energy involved for these inputs. However, resultantly the yields per hectare of crops with traditional farming are very low.

In transitional phase of agriculture, there is a substitution of indigenous practices the cultivation is carried out with the use of some intermediate inputs, animate energy sources, served with irrigation procedures dependent on gravity-style practices and the use of threshers for post-harvest operations. Therefore, the use of commercial energy, especially for machinery and fertilizer, increases sharply.

In modern agricultural systems, the practices involve a shift to a package of improved inputs to achieve greater levels of output, other energy inputs are used to enhance the solar energy transformations. These include the use of tractor's, diesel pump sets and other improved machinery, and an increased reliance on high doses of chemical fertilizers and the application of pesticides etc. This modern technology incorporated in agriculture is energy-intensive and is usually referred to in most of the developing countries as the "Green Revolution".

Summation of all of the these energy values of the inputs incorporated in an individual farming system specify the non-solar energy requirements of the total amount in crop production in an unit area.

ENERGY ANALYSIS IN AGRICULTURE

Energy assessment in agriculture can be made by taking into account the whole system of agriculture (crop and animal) or for a specific crop production. In case of crop and animal production, the entire system has to be considered and energy balance of total inputs and output is evaluated. For this, energy analysis is done to work out the efficiency of various sub-systems within the same environment.

The concept of energy analysis and energy efficiency in any production system relates to the input and output of energy. The purpose and function of energy analysis is to consider the amount of energy required to manufacture a good or create a service which may be computed taking into account both direct and indirect energy use. Critoph (1981) defines energy analysis as the systematic tracing of energy flow through (in industrial) system apportioning the quantity of primary energy input required to produce some output commodity. Leach (1976) states, that the major aim of energy analysis is to estimate the total quantity of energy required directly or indirectly to provide a good or service to a final user. This he has termed as Gross Energy Requirement (GER), or briefly as 'energy input'. The energy input or GER is the fuel value of all non-solar inputs, direct and indirect, to the crop production system i.e., excluding transport and processing of the harvested products. In addition to gross measures of energy consumption in a system, there are three general classes of derived measures : energy efficiency, energy intensity and energy density.

Energy efficiency

Energy efficiency is related to the ratio of input to output of energy in food systems i.e., the returns to energy invested. If output of energy exceeds input the process is described as 'efficient' and if input 'exceeds' output, the process is described as 'inefficient'. Energy ratio* is the ratio between total energy in output and that in input. Energy output divided by energy input gives the simple energy efficiency measure.

---

* Energy Ratio (ER) is defined as the ratio of the metabolizeable energy in the food produced divided by total amount of primary energy in the ground that had to be extracted in order to manufacture all the inputs to the farming process (or the fossil energy in).

Er = Energy Output/Energy input

where,

Er is the Efficiency ratio.

Just as an input-output ratio in monetary terms measures economic efficiency, and that in ecosystem, energy terms measures ecological efficiency. And in crop production, it can be obtained in the form of a ratio of energy in the edible yield of the crops to the energy expanded for the production of edible yield (Bala *et al.*, 1989). When the quantity of product per unit energy is required for its production is considered it denotes energy productivity. In agricultural terms, energy productivity is simply the quantity of an agricultural or food product produced, divided by the summation of all primary energy inputs required for its production (with convenient unit of expression kJ/kcal per kg.). The concept of energy balance in the system implies – inflows and outflows through production, trade etc., and how the energy budget is balanced? When crop and animal production system is considered, and energy balance of total inputs and output is evaluated, energy efficiency of individual sub-systems can be worked out.

Energy intensity

It refers to the amount of energy used per unit of output. To measure energy intensity or energy cost, the output may be considered in a form of commodity, fiscal or in the case of transportation, weight × distance unit.

Energy consumption density

It refers to the consumption of energy per unit area. In the context of crop cultivation, it is the amount of energy to be evaluated per hectare of cultivated land.

Energy analysis of different crops in different regions and under different technologies show the nature of energy consumption in accordance with different operations and sources. The analysis can also be attempted for a particular period and over a series of years to evaluate the growth of energy intensity and productivity of energy.

REFERENCES

Bala, *et al.* (1989). Energy Use Pattern of an Electrified Village in Bangladesh, *Energy*, Vol. 14, No. 2, pp. 61-65.

Critoph, R., (1981). Energy Analysis. In : *Energy – Present and Future Options*, Vol. 1 (eds. D. Merrick and R. Marshall), New York, p. 303.

Leach, G., (1976). *Energy and Food Production*, IPC, Science and Technology Press, Guildford.

Newcombe, K., (19976). The Energetics of Vegetable Production in Asia, Old and New, *Search*, Vol. 7, No. 10, Oct., p. 423.

2

Measurement of Energy Efficiency in Food Production Systems

Review of the Literature

One of the earliest attempts to study the use of energy in agriculture, Odum (1967) tried to present an approximate analysis of energy relations within a semi-pastoralist economy system of Dodo tribe of Uganda. The study highlights, that under the cultivation system, most of the food produced and consumed in terms of grains is more than five times the amount of cultural energy invested. The farming system yielded food energy at a ratio of 2.9 times the cultural energy invested.

Black (1971) computed energy ratio, which he termed as 'Energy Ratio' (ER) to the industrialized agricultural production system by selecting certain energy inputs used indirectly and the amount of fuel consumed by the tractors when used in operations. He concluded, that the industrialized agriculture was no more efficient in any way in energy use than the manual power or draught animals used in cultivation. In other words, which may appear much more productive than primitive methods, are probably very similar in terms of efficiency with which the total energy resources are committed.

Rappaport (1971) measured the flow of energy on garden plots scattered along the east bank of the Simbai river in the central highlands of the Australian Trust Territory of New Guinea. That system of farming (gardening) is called 'Swiddening' and the farmers who follow the farm practices belong to Tsembaga—a local group of people, speaking 'Maring' language. The study systematically considers a number of operations that are followed for the cultivation of staple crops like, taro and sweet potato, and the starchy vegetables like, yam, cassava and banana. For each operations i.e., burning and weeding out the natural growth, for planting of crops, and for their weeding, harvesting and transportation; the energy values were assigned in kcal/acre and thus a ratio of yield to input for individual crop was calculated.

Dekkers *et al.* (1974) analysed the energy relations in Dutch agriculture by selecting certain direct and indirect energy inputs used in three different sectors of agriculture – primary (cereal crops, potatoes, beets, etc., grasses and green fodder); secondary (milk, meat and egg); and horticulture (vegetables and fruits and flowers etc.). The entire exercise for the analysis was made to compute kcal/ha/year.

Stanhill (1974) made an attempt to analyse the use of energy in Israel's agriculture and evaluated agricultural production for both primary and secondary animal products in terms of kcal/year, and thus finally assessed the energy balance of agriculture.

Cervinka *et al.* (1975) in a study of Californian agriculture determined the energy flows by estimating the fuels and electricity requirements. The use of individual fuel was considered in the form of gasoline, diesel fuel, LP gas, aviation gasoline, and natural gas. Energy requirements included for: (a) fertilizer production and distribution, (b) irrigation pumping, (c) crop production, (d) livestock husbandry, (e) transport of farm products to processing plants, (f) initial processing and storage of agricultural products, (g) operation of agricultural aircraft, (h) frost protection, (i) operation of vehicles for farm business, (j) greenhouse heating and ventilation. Estimates of energy use on-farm were developed for three stages of crop production—crop establishment, cultural operations, and harvest for 12 major field crops, 12 major vegetable crops and 12 major fruit and nut crops.

Singh and Chancellor (1975) carried out surveys in seven villages of Meerut district in the state of Uttar Pradesh for the assessment of inputs and outputs which spread over on 500 crop plots belonging to 26 farmers. The surveys were conducted to assemble the details of items of energy inputs, the farmers using under various levels of mechanical technology. The farms were grouped into six distinct categories on the basis of the degree of mechanization and mechanical technology adopted: farms cultivated under rainfed condition, if irrigated – canal and Persian wheel constitute the major source, and having man and animal energy sources only; farm with most or all crop land irrigated by Persian wheel, and having man and animal energy sources only; farms using an electric motor or diesel engine for irrigation, and using human and animal energy for all other production activities; farms using an electric motor or diesel engine to power an irrigation pump as well as to power other machines like wheat thrashers, cane crushers, and maize shellers; farms having a tractor (and no electric motor or diesel engine) used to power an irrigation pump and other stationary machines, along with tillage and transportation activities; and farms having a tractor and using it mainly for tillage and transportation activities, and having an electric motor or diesel engine to power an irrigation pump and other stationary machines. The energy inputs (hp./hr. and kwh) to crop cultivation were substantiated by the cost of individual input and the yield of crop per hectare.

Pimentel *et al.* (1975) while considering the relationship between the consumption of fossil fuel energy and the food protein evaluated the relation in the context of vegetable and animal protein energy. The study highlights fossil energy (including fertilizer, machinery, fuel, and others), land, pumped irrigated farms, and from crop production (seed production, crop establishment, cultural practices, irrigation, fertilizer and harvesting), processing (removal of grains from cob, washing and retorting etc.), packing transportation, marketing (wholesale and retail), shopping, and home preparation. For each of the operation involved, they have calculated the energy inputs in kcal and the specific ratios realized comparing with the output.

Chancellor and Goss (1976) have taken a worldwide view of various scenarios as population growth a facts with food production capabilities dependent on limited land and fossil energy resources. Considering 1975 as the base year, projections were made upto 2000 A.D. with regard to the increase of population, food and energy availability in developed and developing countries of the world. Finally, they have indicated a future possible state of balance in the context of food and energy to sustain the population that would increase by 2000 A.D.

The Food and Agriculture Organisation (1976) made a preliminary examination to evaluate the use of energy in agriculture in the developing countries, and continued its efforts to expand the task in a more elaborative way to present a comprehensive assessment of the use of energy in agriculture for different market economies at the world level (FAO, 1976). As the main aim of the study was to present a world picture, but it also covered some of the developing countries wherever, it was possible. The study consisted the role of commercial energy and use of chemical fertilizers, farm machinery, irrigation equipment, pesticides and labour as the prime resources used for crop production in the developed and developing economies of the world. These resources are inter-correlated and each one of them can partly be substituted for the other. For example, the amount of fossil energy can reduce labour power and *vice versa*. Increasing the land management through various energy inputs (such as fertilizers and tractors) can reduce the land needed, and the approach can be restricted. The accounting procedures used in the analysis are based on the relationships among land, labour and energy.

Spedding and Walsingham (1975) are concerned with the intensive farms of agriculture and the support energy in crop production in the form of fuels, fertilizer and machinery. To them, yield of crops has been substantially increased by the use of non-solar energy inputs rather than the energy derived directly from solar radiation...... "it is the energy use rather than energy flow that matters in agriculture : this includes the amounts used; where they are used......, and the efficiency with which energy is used in the productions."

Brown and Batty (1976) estimated energy allocations in the food system of U.S.A. by considering the energy inputs Kernel Corn No. 303 (1-lb can of whole) with a digestible energy content of 269 kcal, from its production to consumption. Estimations of energy inputs ranged from non-irrigated of preliminary estimates of the commercial energy (which either involve a technology of energy convention or enter commercial channels) consumed in the production and use of chemical fertilizers, farm machinery, irrigation equipments and pesticides, its share at different levels of development and accounting of main energy intensive inputs in the agriculture of each of the main regions of the world. The study incorporates a particular attention to the possibilities for economizing these inputs in their use, and a discussion of the energy requirements of the whole food chain, including processing, transport, marketing and food preparation, besides production itself.

Handreck and Martin (1976) surveyed a number of farms on Yorke Peninsula and in the Murray Mallee of South Australia. Farms in both areas typically were engaged in producing wheat, barley and rearing sheep for wool, cattle and pigs in a flexible rotation of crop, pasture and fallow. The aim of the survey was to assess the energy efficiency of 'typical' cereal/grazing properties run as family farms, those run as stud farms or dairy farms and those operating on a share-farming basis, or raising large numbers of pigs, were excluded. Energy efficiency ratios were computed from the estimates of input and output energy.

Newcombe (1976) in his study of energy use in the Hong Kong food system attempted to evaluate the impact of western technology on the energetic efficiency of the food system by using an energy accounting methodology to examine the energy requirements of crop production and its distribution.

Phipps *et al.* (1976) analysed the energy output/input relationship for forage maize and intensive grassland at the National Institute for Research in Dairying, Shinfield, Reading, Great Britain. For analyzing the above relationship, they considered number of man-hours, amount of diesel fuel/ha./year, machinery, seed, herbicides and fertilizers and their energy equivalents used for computing the energy values.

In an exhaustive study White (1976) has attempted to analyse various aspects of energy use in agriculture and a number of commodities of the United Kingdom. His accounting of energy in case of inputs ranges from the solid fuels to the imported feed stuffs and for output from arable crops to horticulture and livestock.

Johnson *et al.* (1977) while considering the energy conservation measures, analysed them with the agriculture of Amish, the natives of U.S.A. and Canada who constitute their number as 70,000 and most of them live in communities in Pennsylvania, Ohio, Indiana, and Illinois. The study was designed to determine : (i) how much less energy the Amish use then their non-Amish neighbours, and (ii) what penalty they pay in reduced yields because of their agricultural methods? Thus the energy use in crop production by the 'Amish' and the 'English' farmers were compared by computing their energy ratios (which is described as the amount of food energy produced per unit of energy spent to produce it).

Craumer (1978-79) evaluated the farm productivity and energy efficiency in the Keshacoquillas Valley (locally called the Big Valley) of Central Pennysalvania north of Lewiston in Mifflin County. This valley is characterized with the dairying activity, and a few crops of maize, small grains and hay are intensively cultivated. The valley is occupied by an Amish group of population, whose number then approximately enumerated as 1,280 persons, on 180 farms, out of an overall population of about 70,000 of Amish groups who live in North America.

Norman (1978) attempted to evaluate the use of energy in subsistence cropping systems in the torpics computing their input-output ratios. He quoted some examples for making comparisons from tropical agricultural systems which are either wholly or partly devoted to subsistence food production. His estimates considered a comparison of : (i) human and animal energy, (ii) hoe and draught animal subsistence farming systems, rainfed and irrigated agriculture, and (iii) cereals and non-cereals (cash crops).

Deleage *et al.* (1979) applied eco-energetics analysis to describe the structure and functioning of the French agricultural system on the basis of two distinct categories of energy inputs and energy value of production in terms of output. Both the categories consisted of items belonging to four distinct groups of inputs : (i) direct energy inputs, (ii) indirect inputs, (iii) human, and (iv) animal work, and imported vegetable products. The direct energy inputs considered were the fossil fuels and electricity; whereas the indirect inputs included the agricultural machines, fertilizers and pesticides, buildings and other infrastructures, irrigation, human and animal workforce accounted for their numbers and working hours, and the value of sustenance at normal metabolic rate i.e., the caloric input ration for workers and animals.

Fluck (1979) worked out the utilization of energy in agricultural production system on the basis of a ratio of the caloric energy contained in food to the energy required to produce the food. He has equated the agricultural productivity with the energy productivity (i.e. the quantity of product per unit of input energy) by assigning a convenient measure of energy productivity—kilogrammes per megajoule (kg/MJ).

Zucchetto and Jansson (1979) studied a modern agricultural system of an island of Gotland, located in the Baltic Sea about 200 km south of Stockholm, Sweden which than had a population of 54,000 persons. The study included the analysis of the energy, economic and ecological inter-relationships for the entire region. A part of the study is presented for the analysis of agricultural sector including the fuel and electricity costs 'on' and 'of' the farm, flow of food and organic energy within the agricultural system, estimates of farm household energy consumption and the impact and costs of agriculture on the environmental question pertaining to quality of water.

Kalra and Arya (1980) while assessing the fossil-energy demands of crop production in a multi-cropped area with small fields engaged to produce a wide variety of crops at IARI Farm, New Delhi examined the energy demands for different types of works. The energy demand assessment related to the monsoon season grown crops of maize, sorghum and millets, and the dry winter season crops of wheat and barley, apart from some seasonal vegetables. The methodology of the study involved an analysis on the basis of maintenance of daily performance records of deployment of different types of power units to different operations for the three successive years period (1975-77), along with the personal observations of the energy demands during the period under consideration. The energy supply is provided by crawler tractors, tractors, electrically operated tubewells and petrol engine powered thrashers, and the manual and animal sources. The performance records were enumerated in hours of power units for different operations.

Wilson and Brigstocke (1980) made an appraisal of energy use in British agriculture during the year 1973 considering the ingradients of energy—solid fuels, petroleum, electricity, fertilizers, machinery, feedstuff processing (off farm), chemicals, buildings, transport services and others. The study takes into account the alternative energy sources, and more specifically the solar energy to supplement traditional forms of power in the foreseeable future.

Johnson (1980) presented principal results for a study on direct and indirect total energy consumption trends in EEC (countries of France, Denmark, United Kingdom and Italy) agriculture and horticulture over the period of 1972-77. The study goes on to assess the likely future trends in the light of energy price rise, given the scope for and initiatives on energy conservation and the use of renewable energy sources and current farm practices.

Edwardson *et al.*(1981) when assessing the energy requirements of novel protein production systems compared them along with an examination of the environmental implications of the systems. While considering the potential of a novel source of human food or livestock feed emphasized that a number of criterian, often inter-related, have to be taken into account. The individual aspects may be the production process, the nutritional value and acceptability of the product environmental factors, the extent of present and projected future demands, and relative ease of marketability in competition with alternative food or feed resources.

McFate (1981-82) attempted to examine the future food supplies and future energy needs with many interacting challenges in United States of America.

Pimentel *et al.* (1983) attempted to examine the energy efficiency, yield performance, and labour requirements for the production of corn, wheat, potatoes, and apples using (without synthetic chemical fertilizers and pesticides) and conventional farming technologies in some selected states of United States of America.

Dazhong and Pimentel (1984) while attempting to evaluate energy inputs in agricultural systems of China analysed the energy inputs in corn, rice, sorghum, wheat, soyabean, and millet in northeastern China in Dawa and Faku counties of Liaoning province, and Hailun county of Heilongjiang province.

Fluck (1984) examined the role of energy as an input to industrialized agriculture in U.S.A. and its interactions with land and other inputs to their more efficient use. He emphasized the conservation of energy which may lead to an increasing energy productivity in production (especially with respect to irrigation, fertilization, processing, transportation, distribution and food preparation.

Hirst (1984) discussed the quantities of energy required to grow, process, transport, wholesale, retail, refrigerate, and cook food in the U.S.A. for the year 1963 and to estimate the annual energy consumption for food during the period 1960 to 1970. He attempted to evaluate the energy requirements per unit of food energy and of food protein for the major food groups.

Han and Mou (1985) have attempted to examine the energy dynamics and productivity of a set of 14 collective farms and agricultural communes in north China using the analytical methods of ecosystems ecology. They selected the Huang-Huai-Hai River Basin of northern China, an area with low to medium agricultural productivity. Data they collected related to a variety of production factors. The study focused on two system measures: the production of agricultural products and the energy input-output relationship of each farm.

Sundarta and Subramanian (1987) have assessed the energy use through various inputs to cropping systems based on short-duration sugarcane and energy output-input ratios were worked out for the crop grown at the Sugarcane Breeding Institute, Coimbatore in India.

Parikh and Syed (1988) presented the methodology and results of the study on estimation of energy consumption in post-harvest food systems in developing countries, on the components of the PHF as: food processing, transportation, storage and cooking, taking into consideration of 70 different processed commodities and 90 countries representing Africa, Latin America, the Far East and Near East.

Joshi (1989) attempted to determine relationships between various energy inputs and output to augment pearl millet productivity and energy use efficiency on some selected farms at the Central Arid Zone Research Institute, Jodhpur.

Mittal and Dhawan (1989) analysed energy parameters for raising crops namely, sugarcane, cotton, paddy, wheat and maize under various irrigation treatments at Ludhiana, Coimbatore and Pantnagar in India.

Thakur and Mishra (1993) conducted a study on energy requirements and energy gaps for production of major crops in Madhya Pradesh, India for the year 1988-89 and 1989-90. They divided the entire state into five major crop zones: (i) rice zone, (ii) rice-wheat one, (iii) wheat zone, (iv) jowar-wheat zone, and (v) cotton-jowar zone.

A sample of 100 households was selected from each crop zone to cover 12 villages from each of 12 districts of the state. The energy use in terms of sources and operations (expressed in hours) were converted into MJ/ha.

Singh *et al.* (1997) while attempting to estimate the use of energy in Indian agriculture have evaluated it in terms of the extent of farm mechanization; human and animal power, mechanical power, stationary power and electric power during Pre-Green Revolution, Green Revolution and Post-Green Revoltion phases.

Saran and Sethi (1999) analysed the energy use pattern in Punjab agriculture by considering different sizes of farms with regard to their efficiency level of technology and energy use pattern. They collected data from primary schedule for three consecutive years i.e., 1991-92, 1992-93 and 1993-94 for principal crops grown in Punjab. The state was divided into three agro-climatic zones :

Zone I : Wheat, paddy and maize cultivated area.
Zone II : Wheat, maize and groundnut cultivated area.
Zone III : Wheat, cotton and bajra cultivated area.

REFERENCES

Black, J.N. (1971). Energy Relations in Crop Production, *Annals of Applied Biology*, Vol. 67, pp. 272-77.

Brown, S.J. and Batty, J.C. (1976). Energy Allocation in the Food System: A Microscale View, *Transactions of the American Society of Agricultural Engineers (ASAE)*, Vol. 19, No. 4, pp. 758-61.

Cirvinca, V. *et al*. (1975). Methods Used in Determining Energy Flows in California Agriculture, *Transactions of the ASAE*, Vol. 18, No. 2, March-April, pp. 246-51.

Chancellor, W.J. and Goss, J.R. (1976). Balancing Energy and Food Production, 1975-2000, *Science*, Vol. 192, No. 4236, 16 April, pp. 213-18.

Craumer, P.R. (1978/1979). Farm Productivity and Energy Efficiency in Amish and Modern Dairying, *Agriculture and Environment*, Vol. 4, pp. 281-99.

Dazhong, W. and Pimentel, D. (1984). Energy Inputs in Agricultural Systems of China, *Agriculture, Ecosystems and Environment*, Vol. 4, pp. 29-35.

Dekkers, W.A. *et al*. (1974). Energy Production and Use in Dutch Agriculture, *Netherlands Journal of Agricultural Science*, Vol. 22, pp. 107-18.

Deleage, J.P. *et al*. (1979). Eco-Energetic Analysis of an Agricultural System : The French Case in 1970, *Agro-Ecosystems*, Vol. 5, pp. 345-65.

Edwardson *et al*. (1981). Energy and Environmental Implications of Novel Protein Production Systems, *Agriculture and Environment*, Vol. 6, pp. 1-21.

Fluck, R.C. (1979). Energy Productivity : A Measure of Energy Utilization in Agricultural Systems, *Agricultural Systems*, Vol. 4, No. 1, Jan., pp. 29-37.

Fluck, R.C. (1984). Energy, Land and Food : Vital Connections, *Energy in Agriculture*, Vol. 3, pp. 267-75.

F.A.O. (1976). Energy for Agriculture in the Developing Countries, *Monthly Bulletin of Agricultural Economics and Statistics*, Vol. 25, No. 2, Feb., pp. 1-8.

Han, C.R. and Mou, Z.G. (1985). Energy Analysis of Advanced Collective Farms in North China, *Agriculture, Ecosystems and Environment*, Vol. 13, pp. 217-40.

Hendreck, K.A. and Martin, A.E. (1976). Energetics of Wheat/Sheep

Farming System in Two Areas of South Australia, *Search*, Vol. 7, pp. 436-43.

Hirst, E. (1984). Food-Related Energy Requirements, *Science*, Vol. 184, pp. 134-38.

Johnson, R.H. (1980). Energy Trends in EEC Agriculture. In : *Energy Conservation and Use of Renewable Energies in the Bio-Industries* (Ed. F. Vozt), pp. 295-306.

Johnson, W.A. *et al.* (1977). Energy Conservation in Amish Agriculture, *Science*, Vol. 198, 28 Oct., pp. 1-6.

Joshi, N.L. (1989). Efficient Use of Energy Inputs in Rainfed Pearl Millet, *Agriculture, Ecosystems and Environment*, Vol. 25, pp. 91-102.

Kalra, M.S. and Arya, Y.C. (1980). Energy Demand of Crop Production in a Multi-Cropped Area, *Energy*, Vol. 5, No. 11, pp. 1163-67.

McFate, K.L. (1981-82). Food and Energy : Challenges and Choices, *Energy in Agriculture*, Vol. 1, pp. 91-98.

Mittal, J.P. and Dhawan, K.C. (1989). Energy Parameters for Raising Crops Under Various Irrigation Treatments in Indian Agriculture, *Agriculture, Ecosystems and Environment*, Vol. 25, pp. 11-25.

Newcombe, K. (1976). Energy Use in the Hong Kong Food System, *Agro-Ecosystems*, Vol. 2, pp. 253-76.

Norman, M.J.T. (1978). Energy Inputs and Outputs of Subsistence Cropping Systems in the Tropics, *Agro-Ecosystems*, Vol. 4, pp. 355-66.

Odum, H.T. (1967). Energetics of World Food Production. In : *The World Food Problem*, Vol. 2, President's Advisory Committee, Washington, D.C., pp. 55-94.

Parikh, J.K. and Syed, S. (1988). Energy Use in the Post-Harvest Food (PHF) System of Developing Countries, *Energy in Agriculture*, Vol. 6, pp. 325-51.

Pimentel, D. *et al.* (1975). Energy and Land Constraints in Food Protein Production, *Science*, Vol. 190, No. 4216, 21 Nov., pp. 754-61.

Pimentel, D. *et al.* (1983). Energy Efficiency of Farming Systems : Organic and Conventional Agriculture, *Agriculture, Ecosystems and Environment*, Vol. 9, pp. 359-72.

Phipps, R.H. *et al.* (1976). A Comparison of the Energy Output/Input Relationship for Forage Maize and Grass Leys on the Dairy Farm, *Agriculture and Environment*, Vol. 3, pp. 15-20.

Rappaport, R.A. (1971). The Flow of Energy in an Agricultural Society, *Scientific American*, Vol. 225, No. 3, Sept., pp. 117-32.

Spedding, C.R.S. and Walsingham, J.M. (1975). Energy Use in

Agricultural Systems, *Span*, Vol. 18, No. 1.

Saran, S.K. and Sethi, K. (1999). A Study of Energy Use Pattern in Punjab Agriculture, *Indian Journal of Regional Science*, Vol. 31, No. 1, pp. 74-88.

Singh, G. *et al.* (1997). Use of Energy in Agriculture and Future Needs, *Proceedings of the Third Agricultural Science Congress*, PAU, Ludhiana, March 12-15, pp. 103-13.

Stanhill, G. (1974). Energy and Agriculture : A National Case Study, *Agro-Ecosystems*, Vol. 1, pp. 205-17.

Sundarta, B. and Subramanian, S. (1987). Energy Input-Output Studies of Some Crop Sequences based on Short-Duration Sugarcane in Relation to the Conventional Sugarcane System in Tropical India, *Agriculture, Ecosystems and Environment*, Vol. 20, pp. 49-57.

Thakur, C.L. and Mishra, B.L. (1993). Energy Requirements and Energy Gaps for Reduction of Major Crops in Madhya Pradesh, *Agricultural Situation in India*, Vol. 48, No. 9, Dec., pp. 665-69.

White, D.J. (1976). Energy Use in Agriculture. In : *Aspects of Energy Conservation* (Eds. I.M. Blair, B.D. Jones and A.J. van Horn), Oxford, pp. 141-76.

Wilson, P.N. and Brigstocke, T.D.A. (1980). Energy use in British Agriculture – A Review of Future Prospects, *Agricultural Systems*, Vol. 5, No. 1, Jan.-Mar., pp. 51-70.

Zucchetto, J. and Jansson, A.M. (1979). Total Energy Analysis of Gotland's Agriculture : A Northern Temperate Zone Case Study, *Agro-Ecosystems*, Vol. 5, pp. 329-44.

3

Agricultural Productivity
Concept and Methods of Measurement

Productivity is not a synonym of fertility. It is more commonly used to express the power of agriculture in an area to produce crops, irrespective of the fact whether that power is due to the bounty of nature or to the efforts of man. Whereas, fertility relates to the soil to provide all the essential plant nutrients in available form and in a suitable balance needed by the plants for sustenance and healthy growth.

Agricultural productivity may be defined as a ratio between the index of total agricultural output and the index of total inputs used in farm production. It is, therefore, a measure of the efficiency of farming with reference to inputs applied in crop production, other things being equal. Stamp (1960), while attempting to measure crop productivity per unit area emphasized, that the areal differences in productivity are the result partly of natural advantages of soil, and partly of farming efficiency. Farming efficiency refers to the properties and qualities of a number of inputs, the manner in which they are combined and utilized by the farmers in crop production.

There are many different concepts in productivity and a number of ways to compute it. The Chairman of the International Commission on Agricultural Typology, Prof. Jerzy Kostrowicki of Warsaw, Poland invited different views on this problem by sending a questionnaire to more than 100 scholars throughout the world, which contained the following two questions :

1. What methods of measuring the intensity of agriculture should be applied in typological studies of various orders?

2. What methods, measures and indices should be used to define land, labour and capital productivity in agriculture in typological studies of various orders ?

About 50 geographers from all over the world responded to it and suggested various approaches for the measurement of intensity and productivity in agriculture. A few opinions of some of them are given in Appendix-I. The Chairman of the Commission while evaluating different views pointed out that a special study for testing various methods and techniques be used in the studies of various scales where needed.

Productivity of agriculture so far has been looked at from different points of views, such as the productivity of land, labour and capital. In a literary sense, they have been referred to as the partial productivity measures.

PRODUCTIVITY OF LAND

Land on a regional or unit basis expresses the yield of crops in terms of agricultural output, and from a national point of view, it is desirable to secure the employment to the greatest number of persons. Measurement of productivity is obviously of prime importance in countries where there is a great pressure of population on agricultural land. In countries where land is limited, the principal means of raising the agricultural production to keep pace with the growth of population and the demand for improved diet of the people is by raising the yield of crops per hectare.

Increasing the productivity of land, however, does not mean only raising the yields of individual crops. It encompasses, the whole output of a farm or region in relation to the total area of farm land, which may be raised by altering the means of production towards more intensive systems of cultivation or devoting the land for the cultivation of higher value crops. The productivity of land may be increased by raising multiple crops in a year on the same land as many of the farmers of Japan, Taiwan, Egypt and India are doing.

PRODUCTIVITY OF LABOUR

Whereas, the productivity of land is of primary importance as the determinant of total food and agricultural production, the productivity of labour is mainly important as a determinant of income of the population engaged in agriculture in a certain region. The involvement of a worker in agriculture may simply be expressed by the hours of work needed to produce a tonne of wheat or cotton. But except where mainly monocultural agriculture is practiced such measurements have a limited meaning, and therefore, labour productivity is more commonly measured by the total agricultural output per unit of labour in a season or year.

Labour input to agriculture may be expressed as the total number of persons engaged or in order to take into account the intensity of labour as the number of man-hours worked in different farming operations. The more refined system of labour productivity measurement in agriculture is value added per man-hour, which is important chiefly in economically advanced countries where it is intended to compare labour productivity in agriculture with that of the income of persons engaged in occupations other than agriculture. That is of less importance in developing countries where there is an abundance of farm labour and where farm workers are seasonally employed except at times of peak labour demand for harvest and post-harvest operations.

Labour productivity in farming has two important aspects. Firstly, it has a profound effect on national prosperity i.e., the per capita national income; secondly, it determines the standard of living of the population engaged in agriculture. National prosperity in the economic perspective to a greater extent is synonymous with relatively a higher output per man-hour. If a country intends to increase its prosperity, it requires : (a) to provide technical assistance to the labour population to increase per capita productivity, and (b) to stimulate a transfer of labour work force from low productivity to high productivity regions on a regular basis.

PRODUCTIVITY OF CAPITAL

Productivity measures of capital in agriculture are complicated to compute and more difficult to interpret. This is largely because of both diversity of farms and diversity of forms, and various needs and purposes for which capital is utilized in agricultural production. Capital involvement in agriculture is meant for the purchase of land, land reclamation, for work on drainage channels, irrigation, livestock purchase, feeds, seeds, fertilizers and manures, purchase of implements and machinery, electricity, lubricants and fuels, crop protection chemicals etc. To meet out the expenses on all of the above, most of the farmers seek the help of institutional finance on a short term and long term basis.

Measurement of Agricultural Productivity

A number of attempts have been made to measure and quantify agricultural productivity in developing and developed countries of the world.

In an earlier attempt while measuring the relative productivity of British and Danish farming Thompson (1926) expressed it in terms of gross output of crops and livestock by selecting seven parameters : (i) the yield per acre of crops, (ii) number of livestocks per 100 acres, (iii) the gross agricultural production or output per 100 acres, (iv) the proportion of arable land, (v) the number of persons employed in farming, (vi) the cost of production expressed in terms of labour wages, rent or interest, and (vii) price relative profitability and general economic conditions.

While presenting a theoretical discussion for computing productivity in agriculture, Ganguli (1938) considered at the first instance the area under crop ‘A’ in a particular unit area forming a part of certain region. This he expressed as a proportion of the total cropped area of all the crops selected. Secondly, he tried to obtain the index number of yield of a crop. This was found by dividing the yield per hectare for the entire region under study as the standard. This yield may be expressed as a percentage and that percentage may be regarded as the index number of yield. Thirdly, the percentage of the area under crop 'A' and the corresponding index number of yield were multiplied. The product thus obtained indicates actually an index of the contribution of the crop 'A' to the productivity of the unit considered.

Kendall (1939) treated crop productivity measurement as a mathematical problem and initiated a system of four coefficients : (a) productivity coefficient, (b) ranking coefficient, (c) money value coefficient and (d) starch equivalent or energy coefficient.

For determining the productivity by the productivity coefficient method involves the use of advanced mathematics, and the money value coefficient and starch equivalent or energy coefficient poses practical difficulties, therefore Kendall looked for a coefficient which might lead to similar results in productivity computation and save a good deal of calculations. He evolved a method of ranking coefficient, the purpose of which is to arrange in sequence any given number of units of area growing the same range of crops and then determine their agricultural efficiency. For the purpose of ranking coefficient, Kendall took the acre yield of ten leading crops in each of the forty-eight administrative counties of England for four selected years. The acre yield of the selected crops were arranged in descending order for each county and the places occupied by each county with respect to the selected crops were then averaged and thus the ranking coefficient indicating agricultural efficiency of each county was obtained. If a county found its place at the top of every ranking list, it would have a ranking coefficient of one, and if it were at the bottom of every list, it would have a ranking coefficient equal to the number of counties, occupying the place in the list.

Stamp (1952) applied Kandall's ranking coefficient method on an international level to determine agricultural efficiency by selecting certain crops grown in some countries of the world.

Huntington and Valkenburg (1952) considered land productivity on the basis of acre yield of eight crops which were very widely grown in Europe. They selected the average yield of eight crops which were very widely grown in Europe. They selected the average yield per acre of each crop for the entire Europe, and assumed 100 as an index, and the specific yield index for each of the country was calculated.

Stamp (1958) suggested another method for measuring agricultural productivity by converting crop production into calories. The caloric intake is a measure of the general health of a person because it determines the amount of energy needed by the human body. The British Medical Association on the basis surveys and enquiry, published a table showing a range of desirable caloric intake among adults, from 2,100 calories a day, for a woman in sedentary occupation to 2,450 calories for a man engaged in active manual work. For children, the desirable intake is given as 800 calories a day for infants under l year, and for teenage boys as 3,400 calories a day. By considering the age structure, occupation, the weight and height of the peoples living under climatic conditions of northwestern Europe, the average of caloric intake comes to 2,460 a day or about 9,00,000 calories per year. Taking the loss in cooking, stamp termed 10,00,000 (one million) as Standard Nutrition Unit (SNU).

Shafi (1967 and 1969) applied Stamp's SNU technique for measuring the agricultural efficiency by selecting certain food crops in each district of India.

Enyedi (1964) while describing geographical types of agriculture in Hungary refers to a formula for measuring crop productivity. The formula would be read thus :

$$\frac{Y}{Y_n} : \frac{T}{T_n}$$

where

Y = the total yield of crop in the unit area

Y_n = the total yield of crop at the national level

T = the total cropped area of the unit of study

T_n = the total cropped, area at the national level

Sapre and Deshpande (1964) suggested a slight improvement in Kendall's 'ranking coefficient' technique by the simple averaged ranks with that of 'weighted average ranks'. This improvement attempts to incorporate the percentage of crop area to the total area of the district as a unit of study. In order to get the weighted ranks, the ranking position of crop 'a' is multiplied by the magnitude of it to the total cropped area. For example, in an unit area A attains rank 5 on the basis of yield for wheat crop, and wheat occupies 33 percent of area of the total cropped land; jowar attains rank 3 and cultivated on 16 per cent of the total cropped land; rice ranks 4 and occupies 30 percent of the total cropped area. Thus, the weighted average of ranks for the above crops would be: (5 × 33) + (3 × 16) + (4 × 30) = 333 divided by the sum of the weights as 333/79 = 4.21. Applying the Kendall's ranking coefficient, it would be worked out as: 5+3+4=12 divided by the number of crops considered as: 12/3 = 4.

Shafi (1965) suggested the measurement of productivity on the basis of agricultural workers engaged in cultivation. Labour productivity can be computed by dividing the agricultural production (in any unit area) by the number of hours or less precisely by the number of persons who worked in agriculture, or a reverse index be applied when it is intended to get the total number of persons engaged per unit of crop production.

Agarwal (1965) suggested Factorial Approach as a measure of agricultural efficiency. In his study of Bastar district in Madhya Pradesh he took a set of number of human controlled factors pertaining to agricultural production. He included the crop superiority, crop commercialization, crop security, land use intensity and power inputs with the exception of environmental factors.

Bhatia (1967) examined the changes and trends of progress during 1953-1963 in agricultural efficiency in the districts of Uttar Pradesh by adopting Ganguli's method and developed an equation that would be read thus :

(i) $$I_{ya} = \frac{yc}{cr} . 100$$

where,

I_{ya} = the yield index of crop a

yc = the average yield of crop in the area

yr = the average yield of crop a in the entire region

and

(ii) $$E_i = \frac{I_{ya.}\,C_a + I_{ya.}\,C_b + \ldots.I_{ya.}\,C_n}{C_a + C_b + \ldots..C_n}$$

where,

E_i = the agricultural efficiency index

I_{ya}, I_{yb} etc. = are the indices of crops considered

C_a, C_b, etc. = the proportion of cropland devoted to different crops.

Sinha (1968) considered Standard Deviation method as the basis of measuring efficiency in Indian agriculture. For this purpose, he selected all of the twenty-five major crops grown in the districts of the country to group them into : cereals, pulses, oilseeds and cash crops, and specific yield of these crops were taken. In case of cash crops, their output in terms of money value (Rs. per hectare) was computed on the basis of prevailing wholesale prices of that commodity. Finally the standard scores obtained were multiplied by the figures of area under cultivation of crops.

Hayami and Ruttan (1970) measured agricultural labour productivity in developed countries (DC's) and less developed countries (LDC's) of the world for three different periods of time-1955 (1952-56 averages), 1960 (1957-62 averages) and 1965 (1962-66 averages) by using Cobb-Douglas, 'Production Function'. They incorporated independent variables as the cause of productivity differences : land, labour, livestock, fertilizer, machinery, education and technical manpower.

Shafi (1972) applied the method initiated by Enyedi, to the Great Indian Plain and concluded that there were certain cases where the results obtained by the formula are influenced by the magnitude of the area under a particular crop when the yield of the district is either the same or is less than the same as the national yield even then the district, by the computation of the formula, has a higher productivity coefficient than that of the national scale.

Example :

Yield of wheat in the district (B) = 15 qnt./ha.

National yield of wheat = 15 qnt./ha.

Area of the district under wheat	=	15,000 ha.
Area under wheat at the national level	=	10,00,000 ha.
Total crop area of the district	=	50,000 ha.
Total crop area at national level	=	5.7 million ha.

Applying the formula :

$$\frac{Y}{Y_n} : \frac{T}{T_n}$$

$$= \frac{2,25,00}{15,00,000} \times \frac{57,00,000}{50,000} = 1.71$$

Productivity coefficient = 171 – 100 = +71 per cent.

The example shows that the district (B) although having the same yield of wheat as the national yield is shown to be 71 per cent more productive which is hardly tenable.

Similarly, there may be a case when the district yield is less than the national yield, but the area under that particular crop whose productivity coefficient is to be determined is more than in the instance cited by Enyedi. In this case too, although the district yield is less, its productivity index would be higher than the national level.

Example :

Yield of wheat in the district (B)	=	12 qnt./ha.
Yield of wheat at the national level	=	15 qnt./ha.
Area under wheat at the national level	=	10,00,000 ha.
Area of wheat in the district	=	20,000 ha.
Area of wheat at the national level	=	10,00,000 ha.

Y = 2,40,000 qnt.

Y_n = 1,50,000 qnt.

T = 50,000 ha.

T_n = 5.7 million ha.

According to the formula the result of the productivity index of the district (C) would be as follows :

$$= \frac{2,40,000}{1,50,00,000} \times \frac{57,00,000}{50,000} = 1.82$$

Productivity coefficient = 182 – 100 = +82 per cent.

It will be seen that although the productivity of the district with regard to wheat is less than that of the national level, the formula shows that the district is 82 per cent more productive than the national level.

Taking the same example which Enyedi has quoted, if only the yield of wheat per hectare is decreased (the yield of wheat in the district per hectare is taken to be less than the figure cited), and other things remain equal, the productivity coefficient of the district again would be higher than the national level.

Example :

Yield of wheat in the district	=	12 qnt./ha.
Yield of wheat at the national level	=	15 qnt./ha.
Area under wheat in the district	=	15,000 ha.
Area under wheat at the national level	=	10,00,000 ha.
Total crop area of the district	=	50,000 ha.
Total crop area at the national level	=	5.7 million ha.

According to the formula the productivity coefficient of the district with respect to wheat

$$= \frac{1,80,00}{1,50,00,000} \times \frac{57,00,000}{50,000} = 1.37$$

Productivity coefficient = 137 – 100 = +37 per cent

It will be seen from the above measurements that in a particular district although the yield per hectare of a crop may be equal to the national level or even less than the national level, the productivity index with respect to that crop is higher than the national level.

Prof. Shafi made an attempt to modify the formula wherein the productivity coefficient of a particular crop may be in conformity with higher or lower yield per hectare of that crop in the district relative to the national level.

In the modified formula the summation of the total yield of all the crops in the district is divided by the total area under the crop considered in the district and the position thus obtained is examined in relation to the total yield of all the crops considered at the national level divided by the total area under those crops. The formula would be read thus :

$$[(y_w/t)+(y_r/t)+(y_m/t)....n] : [(Y_w/T)+(Y_r/T)+(Y_m/T)....n)]$$

or

$$\frac{\sum^{n} y}{t} : \frac{\sum^{n} Y}{t}$$

where,

y_w, y_r, y_m...n = total yield of various crops in the district;
Y_w, Y_r, Y_m...n = total yield of various crops at the national level;
t = total area under different crops in the district;
T = total area under different crops at the national level.

Singh (1972) has evolved a new technique for the measurement of agricultural efficiency, which consists of the measurement of carrying capacity per unit area in terms of population in relation to output per unit area. The method would be read in the equation form as :

(i) $$C_p = \frac{C_o}{S_n}$$

where,

C_p = carrying capacity;
C_o = calorie output per square mile;
S_n = Standard nutrition for ingestion in calories per person/annum

(ii) $$I_{ae} = \frac{C_{pe}}{C_{pr}} \times 100$$

where,

I_{ae} = the index number of agricultural efficiency of an enumeration unit;

C_{pe} = the carrying capacity in terms of population in the component enumeration unit;

C_{pr} = the carrying capacity in the entire region.

The Indian Society of Agricultural Statistics in its 30th Annual Conference held at Bhubaneswar, Orissa, India, discussed some aspects on agricultural productivity in the Indian context. Raheja *et al.* (1977) have measured the impact of high-yielding varieties based on data collected under the scheme, 'Sample Surveys for Assessment of High-yielding Varieties Programme', during 1973-74 and regional variations in productivity on the basis of yield per hectare in India.

Singh *et al.* (1977) have accounted the level of increase in the yield of different crops during three decennial years, i.e., 1950-51, 1960-61 and 1970-71 in each state of India, considering the relationship between the output of foodgrains and related inputs like, the application of fertilizer, proportion of area sown more than once, and gross irrigated area.

Nangia *et al.* (1977) conducted a field study in the village Khandewala, of Haryana state. The study takes into account the productivity levels at different fields of the village in terms of money value during 1974-75 and a number of factors enumerated in three broad categories, viz., environmental, technological and institutional which hold responsibilities for the productivity variations.

Bhalla (1978) has considered output per person on constant average price for measuring productivity of labour in Indian agriculture in order to account for nineteen crops during the trienniums 1962-65 and 1970-73 for each district of the country (India).

Singh (1979) devised a method of presenting a two-dimensional picture of agricultural productivity comprising two components, viz., intensity and spread considering three variables: (i) yield, (ii) grain equivalent, and (iii) cropping system in the districts of Andhra Pradesh state. Accordingly, a relative share of intensity and spread for each micro unit (district) has been computed to the macro unit (state) separately for the above three variables with the help of equations that have been derived.

REFERENCES

Agarwal, P.C. (1965). Measurement of Agricultural Efficiency in Bastar District : A Factorial Approach. *Proceedings of the Summer School in Geography*, Nainital (Unpublished), Department of Geography, A.M.U., Aligarh.

Bhalla, G.S. (1978). Spatial Patterns of Agricultural Labour Productivity, *Yojana*, Vol. 22, No. 3.

Bhatia, S.S. (1967). Spatial Variations, Changes and Trends in Agricultural Efficiency in Uttar Pradesh – 1953-1963, *Indian Journal of Agricultural Economics*, Vol. 22, No. 1, pp. 66-80.

Enyedi, G.Y. (1964). Geographical Types of Agriculture. In : *Applied Geography in Hungery* (ed. M. Pecsi), Budapest, p. 61.

Ganguli, B.N. (1938). *Trends in Agriculture and Populaiton in the Ganges Valley*, London, p. 93.

Hayami, Y. and Ruttan, V.W. (1970). Agricultural Productivity Differences Among Countries, *The American Economic Review*, Vol. 65, No. 5, pp. 895-911.

Kendall, M.G. (1939). The Geographical Distribution of Crop Productivity in England, *Journal of the Royal Statistical Society*, Vol. 162.

Kostrowicki, J. (1966). Principles, Basic Notions and Criteria of Agricultural Typology, *IGU Commission for Agricultural Typology*, Warsaw (Mimeographed).

Nangia, S. *et al.* (1977). Variations in Field Productivity – A Case Study of Khandewala, Haryana, *Occasional Papers No. 7*, Centre for the Study of Regional Development, Jawaharlal Nehru University, New Delhi.

Raheja, S. *et al.* (1977). Factors Contributing to Regional Variations in Productivity and Adoption of High-Yielding Varieties of Major Cereals in India, *Journal of the Indian Society of Agricultural Statistics*, Vo 29, No. 1, pp. 112-13.

Shafi, M. (1965). Approaches to the Measurement of Agricultural Efficiency, *Proceedings of the Summer School in Geography*, Naini Tal (Unpublished), Department of Geography, A.M.U., Aligarh.

——, (1967). Food Production Efficiency and Nutrition in India, *The Geographer*, Vol. 14, pp. 23-27.

——, (1970). Measurement of Food Crop Productivity in India, *Presidential Address*, Indian Council of Geographers, Indian Science Congress, Kharagpur.

——, (1972). Measurement of Agricultural Productivity of the Great Indian Plains, *The Geographer*, Vol. 19, pp. 7-9.

Singh, D. et al. (1977). Crop Productivity Variations in India, *Journal of the Indian Society of Agricultural Statistics*, Vol. 29, No. 1, pp. 113-15.

Singh, J. (1972). A New Technique for Measuring Agricultural Efficiency in Haryana, India, *The Geographer*, Vol. 19, No. 1, pp. 14-27.

Singh, V.R. (1979). A Method for Analysing Agricultural Productivity. In : *Agriculture and Food Supply in Developing Countries* (ed. J.T. Coppock), Published for the Commission on World Food Problems and Agricultural Productivity of the IGU, Department of Geography, University of Edinburg, pp. 143-51.

Stamp, L.D. (1952). The Measurement of Agricultural Efficiency with Special Reference to India, Indian Geographical Society, *Silver Jubilee Souvenir*, Volume, pp. 177-78.

——, (1958). The Measurement of Land Resources, *The Geographical Review*, Vol. 48, No. 1, pp. 110-16.

——, (1960). *Our Developing World*, London, p. 108.

Valkenburg, S.V. and Held, C.C. (1952). *Europe*, p. 102.

4

Energy use in Agriculture in Developed and Developing Countries of the World

According to Food and Agriculture Organization about 1817×10^{12} kcal of commercial energy (181.7 million tonnes of oil equivalent) was consumed in world agriculture in 1972-73. The share of agriculture in total commercial energy consumption was very small; about 3.5 per cent in developed countries and 4.8 per cent in the developing countries (Stout, 1979, and FAO, 1981). The per hectare consumption of total commercial energy in the developing countries varied from 0.2×10^6 kcals in Africa to 1.0×10^6 kcals in Latin America with an average of 0.53×10^6 kcals for all the developing countries taken altogether. This is to be contrasted with an average figure of 5.93×10^6 Kcals for all the developed countries.

At the world level, agriculture's share was estimated as 4.2 per cent for developed countries and 5 per cent for developing countries in 1982 (Table 4.1).

The developed countries as a whole (with 4.1 per cent) were very close to the world average in 1972 because they accounted for 83 per cent of commercial energy used in agriculture. Agriculture's share of total commercial energy used in developing countries was higher (4.9%), but it accounted for only 17 per cent in world agriculture. A decade later, even more rapid growth in energy used in agriculture in developing countries took agriculture's share of total energy used to 6.5 per cent compared with 4.6 per cent in the developed countries. As a consequence, the proportion of energy used in agriculture in developing countries increased to nearly 27 per cent by 1982. During this ten-year period, agriculture's share of total energy fell only in the Near

East, because of the rapid urban and industrial development in the region is increased marginally in Africa, surged ahead in the ACPE and most pronounced of all, in the Far East (6.5 to 14.1 per cent of total energy used). Meanwhile, agriculture's share of total commercial energy used changed little in North America, Eastern Europe and the former countries of USSR, rose by a quarter in Western Europe but declined by nearly a third in Oceania. Table 4.2 shows the total commercial energy used in agricultural production and share of individual inputs in 1972 and 1982 in developed and developing countries of the world.

Table 4.1: Use of Commercial Energy, Total and in Agricultural Production, 1972 and 1982

	Total		*Energy used in agricultural production*			
	1972	*1982*	*1972*	*1982*	*1972*	*1982*
	(M.Tonnes, oil equivalent)				*(in per cent)*	
Developing market economies	413	730	22	45	5.3	6.1
Africa	34	51	2	3	5.0	5.4
Far East	135	147	9	21	6.5	14.1
Latin America	187	298	7	11	3.8	3.8
Near East	54	232	4	10	7.4	4.3
Others	1	3	–	–	3.8	2.0
ACPE	276	444	12	32	4.3	7.2
Total developing countries	689	1175	34	77	4.9	6.5
Developed market economies	3066	3109	120	154	4.2	4.9
North America	1763	1668	68	66	3.9	4.0
Oceania	53	82	3	4	6.5	4.4
West Europe	954	1004	52	68	5.4	6.8
Others	296	354	6	16	2.1	4.6
Eastern Europe and USSR	1080	1474	40	57	3.7	3.8
Total developed countries	4146	4583	169	210	4.1	4.6
World	4835	5758	202	287	4.2	5.0

Sources : UN, *Energy Stati stics Yearbook, 1982,* (N.Y., 1984)*; and FAO estimates.*

Table 4.2: Aggregate Commercial Energy used in Agricultural Production—Share of each Input in 1972 and 1982

(*in percentage*)

	Total		*Farm machinery*		*Fertilizer*		*Irrigation*		*Pesticides*	
	1972	*1982*	*1972*	*1982*	*1972*	*1982*	*1972*	*1982*	*1972*	*1982*
	Millions tonnes oil equivalent									
Developing market economies	22	45	32.5	32.4	60.3	61.3	6.3	4.9	1.0	1.4
Africa	2	3	46.4	41.0	47.0	49.2	4.9	4.2	1.5	5.5
Far East	9	21	17.4	21.9	75.0	71.4	7.1	6.9	0.4	0.7
Latin America	7	11	46.2	40.3	50.4	56.2	1.7	1.4	1.7	2.1
Near East	4	10	34.6	42.9	51.4	49.1	13.2	6.8	0.8	1.1
ACPE	12	32	17.5	15.7	70.9	79.3	7.1	3.0	4.5	2.0
Total developing countries	34	77	27.2	25.5	64.0	68.8	6.6	4.1	2.2	1.7
Developed market economies	129	154	68.9	68.4	28.5	29.1	0.9	1.0	1.7	1.5
North America	68	66	71.9	66.8	25.2	29.7	1.1	1.4	1.9	2.1
Oceania	3	4	73.8	72.2	74.9	76.4	0.9	1.0	0.5	0.4
West Europe	52	68	65.7	66.4	32.0	31.6	0.6	0.6	1.6	1.3
Eastern Europe and USSR	40	57	47.6	44.9	49.5	52.7	0.8	0.8	2.1	1.6
Total developed countries	169	220	63.9	62.1	33.4	35.5	0.9	0.9	1.8	1.5
World	202	287	57.8	52.3	38.5	44.3	1.8	1.8	1.9	1.6

Source : F.A.O. *The State of Food and Agriculture 1985*, p. 70.

ENERGY USE IN AGRICULTURE IN DEVELOPED COUNTRIES

Energy use in United State's Agriculture

Farming in developed countries use energy mostly in the form of fossil-fuels. The highly mechanized Untied State's farming uses 16.5 per cent of the total energy use of the country. Out of the total of 16.5 per cent, about 18 per cent is used for crop production, 33 per cent for food processing, 3 per cent for transportation, 16 per cent for retail and wholesale marketing and 30 per cent for preparations. About 3 per cent of U.S. energy is used on farms for food production.

Fuel, fertilizer and electricity accounted for the bulk of on-farm energy used to share 45.16, 41.6 and 13 per cent respectively) in U.S. farming (Pimentel 1975 and 1981). On-farm energy use in agriculture increased four-fold from 1940 to 1980, whereas energy use in food system increased five-fold. For maize crop during different points of time 1945, 1970 and 1980, the energy ratios declined from 3.15 (in 1945), 2.69 (in 1970) and 3.08 (in 1980).

There has been a four-fold reduction in labour force (1920-70) and forty-fold increase in mechanical power in U.S. agriculture. This decrease of labour force reflects a decrease in man-hours per hectare for the production of maize which was 57 man-day hours (in 1945) and that came down to 22 man-day hours (in 1970) and 12 man-day hours (in 1980). In between the years 1945 and 1970, the yield of maize increased to about 2.5 fold. About 1 kcal of fossil-fuel is needed to grow 3 kcal of food, which is equal to 1 litre of oil to 9 kg. maize output.

Table 4.3 shows the energy use (operationwise) in different crops grown in U.S. It is evident from Table 4.3 that maize consumes the largest amount of energy which is followed by luzerne and wheat.

Table 4.3: Energy Consumption in some Crops in U.S.A.

(in percentage)

Operation	*Maize*	*Winter wheat*	*Luzerne*	*Soyabean*
Land preparation	5.5	13.2	2.4	16.9
Seeds	1.6	3.1	0.7	5.5
Fertilizing	49.1	46.1	6.7	12.8
Pesticides	3.3	0.4	0.2	8.5
Irrigation	9.1	12.7	24.4	1.3
Harvesting	4.7	5.3	28.3	7.4
Transport	14.4	17.4	23.3	32.6
Drying	10.0	–	12.9	1.8
Electricity	0.1	0.6	0.3	0.7
Others	2.2	1.2	0.8	12.5
Total	100.0	100.0	100.0	100.0
Energy consumption (10^6 kcal/ha.)	4.78	1.90	2.85	1.47

Source : Pimentel, D. *et al.*, "Food Production and the Energy Crisis", *Science*, Vol. 182, 1973, p. 445.

An another study of Energetic Analysis of Missouri Crop Farms on the basis of detailed farm records of Northwest Missouri crop enterprises provided by the University of Missouri's Mail in Record Programme (MIR) was conducted by Schahczenski (1985). The energetic analysis for three crop production systems for corn, soyabean and wheat were made for individual years from 1973 to 1982. Energy Productivity Ratios (EPR) were computed and percentage changes in the trends of EPR between 1973 and 1982 thus determined were to the tune of 22 per cent for corn, 26 per cent for soyabean and 36 per cent for wheat (Table 4.4).

Table 4.4: Energy Productivity Summary Estimates of Missouri Farms in U.S.A.

Year	*Number of systems*			*Average energy used (10^3 MJ)*			*Average output (10^3 kg)*			*EPR (kJ/Mg)*		
	C	*B*	*W*	*C*	*B*	*W*	*C*	*B*	*W*	*C*	*B*	*W*
1973	45	43	15	1484	834	196	660	259	66	0.45	0.31	0.34
1974	53	51	18	1690	857	225	834	210	80	0.49	0.25	0.36
1975	45	47	24	1361	875	145	509	239	97	0.37	0.27	0.67
1976	52	52	34	1609	896	228	573	213	126	0.36	0.24	0.55
1077	51	52	32	1581	929	253	643	337	141	0.41	0.36	0.56
1978	50	51	6	1237	1148	165	591	369	69	0.47	0.32	0.42
1979	48	49	16	1571	1397	272	879	461	170	0.56	0.33	0.63
1980	48	49	23	1384	1161	236	489	370	158	0.35	0.32	0.67
1981	49	51	36	1509	1399	424	863	507	283	0.57	0.36	0.67
1982	41	28	38	1663	1455	354	842	456	141	0.51	0.31	0.40

Source : Schahczenski, J.J., Energetic Analysis of Missouri Crop Farms, *Energy in Agriculture*, Vol. 4, 1985, p. 2

Energy use in Agriculture of United Kingdom

In order to examine energy use in United Kingdom, the cultivation of potatoes has a better performance than U.S. The energy ratio for potatoes is 2.3 in U.K. against 1.6 in U.S. In case of hay and milk, and also in case of wheat U.K. has a higher energy ratio 3.4 for U.K. and 2.0 for U.S. In vegetable cultivation, 1.5 kcal of energy is required to produce 1 kcal of food. For the sake of animal protein production is expensive, wherein the forage crops and grain (about 90 per cent produced) are grown and consumed by livestock to produce milk and meat.

Phipps *et al.* (1976) examined the energy output/input relationships for forage maize and compared it with intensive grassland of the National Institute for Research in Dairying, Shinfield, U.K. The study took into account the diesel fuel, machinery involved in establishment and harvesting, and the fertilizer consumed. For the production of maize 628 kg/ha of a compound fertilizers with an energy equivalent of 20 MJ/kg were used. The grass ley received an initial seed-bed application of 251 kg/ha of compound fertilizer with an energy equivalent of 14 MJ/kg. Most of the nitrogen applied was ammonium nitrate which has a value of 26.2 MJ/kg. From Table 4.5 it is clear, that grassland of NIRD, U.K. required more energy/ha/year than forage maize.

Table 4.5: Energy Inputs (MJ/ha/yr) for the Production of Forage Maize and Intensive Grassland

	Maize	*% of total*	*Grass leys*	*% of total*
Establishment				
Fuel	2,477	11	1,264	4
Fertilizer	—	—	1,171	3
Harvesting				
Fuel	3,408	16	9,093	26
Fertilizer	12,560	59	20,150	58
Seeds	1,377	6	459	1
Herbicide	341	2	44	<1
Machinery and repairs	1,237	6	2,474	7
Total	21,400		34,725	

Source : Phipps *et al.*, "A Comparison of the Energy Output/Input Relationship for Forage Maize and Grass Leys on the Dairy Farm", *Agriculture and Environment*, Vol. 3, 1976, p. 17.

Energy use in French Agriculture

Table 4.6 shows the energy consumption in French agriculture, wherein the energy requirement has increased from 15.19×10^{12} to 140.83×10^{12}. A significant increase is in case of direct energy use in agriculture from 28.2 to 51.3 per cent. If overall energy efficiency is considered, the ratio was 1.37 (in 1960) which declined 1.03 in 1975.

Table 4.6: Energy Consumption in French Agriculture

	1945	*1960*	*1975*
Direct : Machinery	6.2	23.0	25.4
Transport	—	2.4	3.8
Drying	6.2	5.0	4.9
Green House	—	1.0	4.0
Animal Rearing	7.8	4.2	2.6
Electricity	4.5	2.1	3.9
Total	28.2	46.6	51.3
10^{12} kcal	(4.28)	(30.84)	(72.31)
Indirect : Pesticides	–	3.8	3.6
Fertilisers	31.3	27.8	27.6
Construction	16.7	8.6	6.8
Irrigation	5.0	1.5	1.5
Others	18.8	10.7	9.3
Total	71.8	53.4	48.7
10^{12} kcal	(10.91)	(35.36)	(68.52)
Total energy requirement	100.0	100.0	100.0
10^{12} kcal	(15.19)	(66.20)	(140.83)
Gross energy requirement (oil import, etc.)			
10^{12} kcal	—	72.01	159.81
Cereal production 10^{12} kcal	—	64.10	115.92
Total production 10^{12} kcal	—	78.83	166.02
Energy efficiency (foodgrains)	—	0.89	0.72
Overall energy efficiency	—	1.37	1.03

Source : *1980 L' Energie en France*, Electricite de France, Paris, 1980.

Energy inputs to different crops show that fertilizers account for from 45 to 50 per cent of total energy input for the crops of wheat, maize and beet root. In case of sugarbeet and topinambour (an energy crop from which alcohol is extracted to run vehicles), the energy inputs are normally high.

A micro level information for the use of energy is available for an area in the southern Alps, Derreumaux (1978). In three villages, one cereal crop in a village, meat and milk in another village, and fruits in third village were analysed for obtaining energy ratios. The values of energy ratio followed : 1.7 (for cereal crop), 0.62 (for meat and milk) and 0.53 (for fruits).

Out of the 22 regions, the Picardie Centre, Pays de la Ivoire, Bretagne, Midi-Pyrennes and Acquitainc, each share of more than 6 per cent of energy consumption in France. The north of the France is known for the cultivation of wheat, and the center and south for vine cultivation.

ENERGY USE IN AGRICULTURE IN DEVELOPING COUNTRIES

The modern agriculture in the developed countries such as the United States, Canada, Britain, Japan and Soviet Union, and in many more is almost completely mechanized. The land holdings are usually of the size of 100 hectares or more because only a small population, nearly 5 per cent is engaged in agriculture. In the developing countries, the land holdings are small. If we consider the situation in India as a representative, it is evident from Table 4.7 that, there were 97.15 million landholdings in total during 1985-86, out of which marginal holdings accounted for 66.17 million (57.80 per cent), 17.92 million (18.42 per cent) as small, 13.25 million (13.60 per cent) semi-medium, 7.91 million (8.20 per cent) medium and 1.92 million (2.00 per cent) as large.

This number has decreased further in the subsequent years. The farmers having landholdings between 1 and 4 hectares cannot be expected to have mechanized farming using tractors or power tillers. Therefore, the use of manual and animal power becomes inevitable consequence, and thus these sources cannot be replaced in near future. However, in many of the developing countries like India, Bangladesh, Sri Lanka, Pakistan and Philippines, we may have the opportunity of comparing different farming systems, such as the bullock operated, tractor-operated and tractor-bullock operated. Many of the mechanized farming systems require several

Table 4.7: Distribution of Number and Area of Operational Holdings in India by Major Size Classes of Holdings in 1985-96

Major Size Classes (area in ha.)	*Number of holdings*		*Area operated*	
	Number of holdings (thousand)	*Percentage*	*Thousand hectares*	*Percentage*
Marginal (Below 1)	56.147	57.8	22042	13.4
Small (1-2)	17.922	18.4	25708	15.6
Semi-medium (2-4)	13.252	13.6	36666	22.3
Medium (4-10)	7.916	8.2	47144	28.6
Large (Above 10)	1.918	2.0	33002	20.1
All size classes	97155	100.0	164562	100.0

Source : *All India Report on Agricultural Census, 1985-86*, Department of Agriculture and Co-operation, Ministry of Agriculture, Government of India, New Delhi, 1992, p. 6.

manual operations, such as seedling, fertilization, weeding, irrigation and harvesting etc.

In their studies Leach (1976), and Pimentel and Pimentel (1979) have attempted to examine differences in energy use in a few crops of corn, wheat and rice in some selected countries. The yield of corn varies from 1000 to 5000 kg./ha among these countries. Although in U.S.A. and U.K. with highly mechanized and energy intensive farming, the yield has reached 5000 kg/hectare, but in India and Mexico on non-mechanized and semi-mechanized farms the yield has been 2500 and 1934 kg/hectare respectively. This gives an energy output/input ratio 2.57 (in U.S.A.), 2.33 (in U.K.), and 5.02 (in India) and 30.6 (in Mexico) respectively (Table 4.8).

Singh *et al.* (1997) studied the role of energy in increasing agricultural productivity in Indian context in three distinct phases : Pre-Green Revolution Phase (1947-1965), Green-Revolution Phase (1965-1975) and Post-Green Revolution Phase (1975 onwards). The study accounted for farm mechanization, farm power (human and animal power), mechanical power (tractive power-tractors and power tillers), stationary power (electric/diesel engines for

Table 4.8: Energy Budgets of Corn Production in Different Countries of the World

Energy GJ/ha/yr

Inputs	*Mexico*	*Guate-mala*	*Nigeria*	*Philp-pines*	*India*	*U.S.A.*	*U.K.*
Labour	0.915	0.561	0.496	0.237	0.119	0.018	–
Animal	–	2.488	–	1.168	0.0224	–	–
Machinery	0.045	1.013	0.045	1.013	0.050	4.343	2.84
Fuel	–	–	–	–	0.346	–	–
Fertilizer	–	–	–	–	–	–	–
Manures							
Organic	–	–	–	–	3.000	–	–
Inorganic	–	–	0.900	0.375	3.820	11.12	5.51
Others	–	–	–	–	–	5.45	14.20
Total	0.960	4.062	1.440	2.790	7.56	29.85	26.37
Output							
Grain (in kg.)	1934	1056	994	931	2500	5060	5002
Grain Energy	29.40	16.05	15.10	14.15	37.9	76.91	61.7
Output (Grain/Input ratio)	30.6	3.95	10.48	5.06	5.02	2.57	2.33
Output (Biomass) Input ratio	80.8	11.2	29.8	14.3	13.3	–	–

Source : *Global Aspects of Food Production* (eds. M.S. Swaminathan and S.K. Sinha), Tycooly, Oxford, 1986, p. 66.

irrigation), electricity and diesel used in agriculture. The study also took a stock of future energy availability scenario and the future energy needs for the period upto 2000—the animate energy needs of 10,269 MJ/ha., and mechanical energy 110,637 Gwh, and the rest of the mechanical energy (976 MJ/ha) which is required can be supplied in the form of 2919 thousand tonnes of diesel to agriculture.

The study of energy use pattern in Punjab agriculture has been attempted by Saran and Sethi (1999) to present a comparison of different sizes of farms, the efficiency levels of technology and energy use pattern. They collected data from primary schedule from Punjab Agricultural University, Ludhiana for three consecutive years i.e., 1991-92, 1992-93 and 1993-94 for principal crops grown in Punjab and three agro-climatic crop zones on the basis of dominance of corps. The Punjab state divided into three zones are: Zone I—wheat, paddy and maize area; Zone II—wheat, maize and groundnut area; and Zone III—wheat, cotton and bajra area.

The sampling design of the study was stratified into three stage random sampling with district as the first stage sampling unit, tehsil (a sub-division of the district) as the second stage unit, and farmer of the selected village as the third unit of study. A total of 30 villages from 27 tehsils of the state were selected, and the farmers were classified according to the size of land holdings as : small farmers—with less than 3 hectares; medium farmers—3-6 hectares; and large farmers—above 6 hectares.

The selection of sample restricted to 300 households. In this way 110 holdings represented Zone I; 90 holdings from Zone II and 100 holdings from Zone III for the period 1991-94.

The study took into account the following parameters: (1) operational land holdings—irrigated and un-irrigated farms, (2) total cropped area and area under individual crops, (3) human labour—family members, permanent worker and causal worker, (4) animal—bullock-hour, (5) tractors—owned or hired, (6) sources of irrigation—canal, electricity and diesel operated pump sets, (7) thrashing/mode of thrashing and quantity, (8) seed rate-quantity (in kg.), (9) farmyard manure-quantity (in qnts.), (10) fertilizers—quantity of NPK (in kg.) and (11) crop production—main product and byproduct (in qnts.).

The study is based on Best Practice Frontier Analysis (BPFA), the purpose of which is to work out the efficiency of farms using a number of energy inputs. The study concluded that, the energy use per hectare varies significantly between different levels of efficiency, between different levels of technology and also according to the size of farm. Per hectare use of commercial (fertilizers, tractors, thrashers and electric/ diesel engine) and non-commercial (human labour, animal and seed) energy decreases with the increase in the level of efficiency among the farms belonging to the categories I and II. In the village farms belonging to category III, per hectare use of commercial and non-commercial energy increased with the increase in the efficiency level. In category IV, per hectare use of commercial energy decreased with the increase in the efficiency of the farms. But per hectare use of non-commercial energy increased from 3469.95 to 4209.85 MJ per hectare from the efficiency group II to efficiency group III.

REFERENCES

FAO (1981). *Agriculture Toward 2000*, Rome.

Derreumaux, Jean-David (1978). Analyse Energetique des exploitations agricoles de trois communes des alpes du sud, CATADAS, les Mecs.

Leach, G. (1976). *Energy and Food Production*, IPC Science and Technology Press, Guilford, U.K.

Phipps, R.H. *et al.* (1976). A Comparison of the Energy Output/Input Relationship for Forage Maize and Grass Leys on the Dairy Farm, *Agriculture and Environment*, Vol. 3, pp. 15-20.

Pimentel, D. and Pimentel, M. (1979). *Food, Energy and Society*, Edward Arnold Ltd., London.

Pimentel, D. (1981). Food, Energy and Environment, *Proceedings of N.S. Institute of Science*, pp. 85-100.

Pimentel, D. *et al.* (1975). Energy and Land Constraints in Food Protein Production, *Science*, Vol. 190, No. 4216, 21 Nov. 1975, pp. 754-61.

Saran, S.K. and Sethi, K. (1999). A Study of Energy Use Pattern in Punjab Agriculture, *Indian Journal of Regional Science*, Vol. 31, No. 1, 1999, pp. 74-88.

Schahczenski, J.J. (1985). Energetic Analysis of Missourri Crop Farms, *Energy in Agriculture*, Vol. 4, pp. 253-69.

Singh *et al.* (1997). Use of Energy in Agriculture and Future Needs, *Proceedings of the Third Agricultural Science Congress-1997*, Vol. I, National Academy of Agricultural Sciences, Punjab Agricultural University, Ludhiana, pp. 103-13.

Stout, B.A. (1979). *Energy for World Agriculture*, FAO, Rome.

5

Energy Use in Food Production System in Aligarh District

In order to assess the judicious use of resources, much attention has been devoted to evaluate various aspects in crop production systems. The entire crop production system can be evaluated in relation to its energy requirements. The basic objective is to ascertain the use of energy and its efficiency in crop production system. In case of individual crops and their related yields, it is not clear that in terms of efficiency the energy-intensive farms are superior or the traditional farms which normally follow less energy-intensive practices.

As the cultivation of crop follows a sequence of a number of agronomic practices, therefore, the mode of energy utilization varies from traditional to transitional, and from transitional to modern. By examining the relationship between the energy-intensive inputs and the relative yields of crops divided, it is easy to identify the relative importance of each of energy-intensive inputs and to evaluate the potential for energy conservation.

The Aligarh District

The district of Aligarh forms a part of the State of Uttar Pradesh with an area of 5,027 sq.km. It is located in a fertile agricultural tract of the Ganga-Yamuna Doab between 27°28'N and 28°11'N latitudes, and 77°29'E and 78°38'E longitudes. It is bounded by the river Ganga on the northeast and by the river Yamuna on the northwest. The district has its greatest width of 112 kilometres from west to east near the northern border from the Yamuna to the river

Ganga, while its maximum length from north to south is 72 kilometres.

Physiographically, the district consists of a vast alluvial plain possessing a gentle slope from north to south and southeast. The entire district presents a level appearance and seems to be almost homogenous in character.

The general topographical features are very similar to that of the Doab and on the basis of the nature of alluvium, it can be divided into two parts : (i) the old alluvium or *bhangar* and (ii) the new alluvium or *khadar*. The former occupies invariably the higher grounds, while the latter occurs on the terraces and flood plains of the rivers and tributaries draining the district. Thus from the low Yamuna flood plains lying in the west, the general slope of the land rises to the high upland in the center. Further east it descends into a depression formed by the river Kali Nadi. From the Kali Nadi further east, the land again rises and finally merges into low lying Ganga flood plains.

The drainage of the district is provided chiefly by the perennial rivers namely, Ganga, Yamuna and Kali Nadi. The other drainage channels like Karon, Sirsa and Nim are ephemeral in character only when there is heavy downpour.

The Aligarh district experiences the tropical monsoon type of climate with a characteristic seasonal rhythm marked by the northeast and northwest monsoons. The entire year is generally divided into four distinct seasons :

(i) Cold weather season (December to February)
(ii) Hot weather season (March to mid-June)
(iii) Season of general rains (Mid-June to September)
(iv) Season of retreating monsoon (October to November)

The alluvial soils of the district are divided into : old (*bhangar*) alluvium and new (*khadar*) alluvium. The old alluvium (*bhangar*) occupies the level plain above the flood-level of the courses of main rivers and their tributaries, while the new alluvium (*khaddar*) is confined to the flood plains of the rivers and their tributaries. These soils differ considerably in their texture and consistency, ranging from sands, loams and silts to heavy clay in the drained areas. The soils are sometimes charged with injurious salts known as *reh*. The drainage of the area exercises a considerable influence upon the distribution and fertility of the soils. From the banks of the river Ganga in the east, for instance the character of the soil varies from sandy to sandy loam and clayey loam upto the middle parts of the district. Moving further west there occurs a sandy-loam tract which finally merges into the sandy bed of the river Yamuna.

Keeping in view the above objectives and to establish the relationship between energy requirements of individual crops grown in a certain system and the output of crops (in terms of energy), and to examine the levels of crop productivity, and to demarcate high, medium and low energy use efficiency regions intensive field surveys were undertaken in 122 selected villages belonging to 17 different developments blocks of 6 tehsils namely, Atrauli, Hathras, Iglas, Khair, Koil and Sikandra Rao of the Aligarh district. A series of 1,137 farmers varying with operational holdings were interrogated (Appendix I).

The basis for the selection of Aligarh district was to study in-depth some of the important characteristics of crop cultivation and examine further the yield of crop in relation to the use of energy in the production process. Moreover, as at official level the required information was not available, first hand information was obtained by interviewing the farmers personally.

A team of staff consisting JRFs initiated survey by visiting the selected villages alongwith an exhaustive questionnaire in each block of different tehsils of the district during the two different crop seasons *kharif* and *rabi* of the year, and the entire process of survey extended over 2 years (1988-89 to 1989-90).

The method of selection of 122 villages (out of 1,704 villages) of the district was on the basis of purposive-clustered sampling from different zones spaced at an interval of 5 km from the district headquarters radiating upto 50 km to cover the entire district (Fig.5.1). Detailed investigations on the basis of a questionnaire (Appendix-II) and the responses of query of the farmers were recorded systematically about the cultivation of crops, the items of energy used, and the output derived in both seasons.

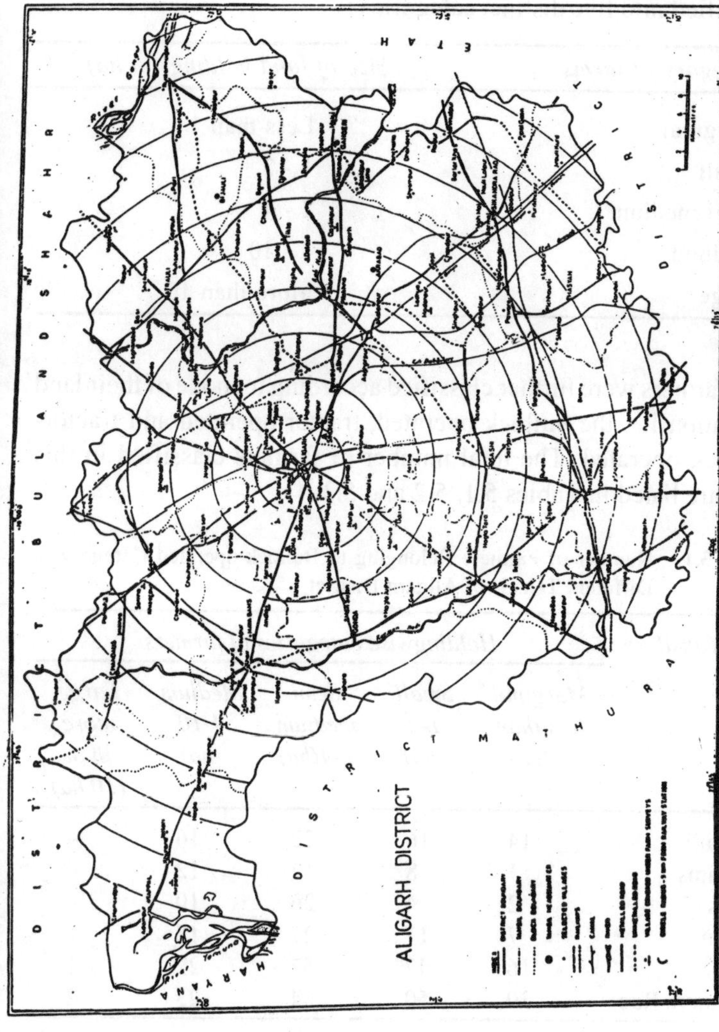

Fig. 5.1: Aligarh District — Showing the Villages Selected for Conducting Field Survey

Methodology Adopted

On the completion of surveys, the total number of farmers were classified into five distinct categories :

Category of farms	*Size of land holding (in ha)*
Marginal	Less than 1
Small	1 - 2
Semi-medium	2 - 4
Medium	4 - 10
Large	More than 10

The farmers were further classified according to mode of their land operation i.e. the bullock operated, tractor operated and tractor-bullock operated. The total number of farmers classified in this way are listed in Tables 5.1, 5.2 and 5.3.

Table 5.1: Number of Farmers Belonging to Bullock-operated Category in Different Tehsils of Aligarh District

Tahsil	*Holdingwise categories of farmers*				
	Marginal less than 1 (ha)	*Small 1-2 (ha)*	*Semi medium 2-4(ha)*	*Medium 4-10 (ha)*	*Large more than (10 ha)*
Atrauli	14	16	22	16	–
Hathras	1	8	12	12	–
Iglas	2	4	26	10	–
Khair	7	17	27	18	–
Koil	16	47	52	22	1
Sikandra Rao	30	50	34	23	2
Total	70	142	173	101	3

The farmers in the selected villages were interviewed by the survey team to collect information pertaining to the items of energy input used in cultivation of a crop, and the output obtained (in terms of yield/ha) by the farmer. While the work of survey in the villages was in progress, there were many instances in each village where the required number of farmers were not found with the same size of land-holdings to tally the above mentioned predetermined categories of land-holdings. To avoid this constraint, it was considered to incorporate the farmers from other categories of land holdings in the village and who were ready to respond to the questions of the survey team.

The data collection was based on pre-harvest and post-harvest operations relating to input in cultivation and output of crop production. The pre-harvest operations included: tilling of land, sowing of seeds, amount of seeds utilized, weeding, watering and application of fertilizers. The post-harvest operations included: harvesting, drying and thrashing, transport and storage.

Table 5.2: Number of Farmers Belonging to Tractor-operated Category in Different Tehsils of Aligarh District

Tahsil	*Holdingwise categories of farmers*				
	Marginal less than 1 (ha)	*Small 1-2 (ha)*	*Semi medium 2-4(ha)*	*Medium 4-10 (ha)*	*Large more than (10 ha)*
Atrauli	8	8	9	8	1
Hathras	17	15	14	7	1
Iglas	12	7	10	11	2
Khair	12	15	1	10	5
Koil	21	28	43	34	5
Sikandra Rao	47	26	15	9	6
Total	117	99	92	79	20

Conversion Factors

An assessment of energy input and output may conveniently be expressed in the common energy measures : Joule, Calorie, Watt, Horsepower-hrs and British Thermal Unit (BTU). These measures can easily be converted from one form to another by incorporating their equivalences.

Table 5.3: Number of Farmers Belonging to Tractor-bullock operated Category in Different Tehsils of Aligarh District

Tahsil	*Holdingwise categories of farmers*				
	Marginal less than 1 (ha)	*Small 1-2 (ha)*	*Semi medium 2-4(ha)*	*Medium 4-10 (ha)*	*Large more than (10 ha)*
Atrauli	4	9	7	4	–
Hathras	4	4	4	7	–
Iglas	7	4	6	9	–
Khair	4	6	8	9	1
Koil	13	22	37	24	1
Sikandra Rao	4	12	7	5	–
Total	36	57	69	58	2

In general term of reference Joule, Calorie and Watt are used in:

10^3	Kilo	K
10^6	Mega	M
10^9	Giga	G
10^{12}	Tera	T
10^{15}	Peta	P
10^{18}	Exa	E

The appropriate equivalences may be :

For example,

1 Joule	=	0.00024 kcal
1 Calorie	=	4.187 J
1 KJ	=	0.24 kcal
1 Kcal	=	4.18 KJ
	=	0.00156 hp-hr
1 Kwh	=	3,600 KJ
	=	861 kcal

	=	1.341 British horsepower
	=	3412.76 Btu
1 Btu	=	1055.06 Joules
	=	252.99 Calories
1 Hp-hr	=	2686.44 KJ
	=	641.61 kcal
	=	2545 Btu
	=	0.74 Kwh

On the basis of extensive surveys the information collected for the inputs and output under individual farm and crop were separately tabulated.

As the energy inputs to individual farm and crop were recorded in physical units on the basis of surveys conducted, it becomes necessary to convert these units into energy units. The norms of conversion which thus were separately developed for bullock operated farms, tractor operated farms and tractor-bullock operated farms. As the agronomic practices vary in pre-harvest and post-harvest operations, therefore, they were developed specifically for a set of operations in both cases.

Pre-determined norms for Bullock operated farms

I. Pre-harvest operations

1. Tilling of land – Tilling by manual and animal operations involves :
1 person + 1 pair of bullock × Area (under crop in ha.) × No. of tilling
= (0.1* + 1.0**) × Area × No. of tilling
= 1.1 × Area × No. of tilling

---

* Human (man-hour) is 0.1 hp, 470 kcal in energy equivalent.

** A pair of bullock (pair-hour) is 1 hp-hrs, 2,420 kcal in energy equivalent.

2. Sowing of crop

(i) Sowing of wheat and barley
3 persons + 1 pair of bullock × Area
= (0.3 + 1.0) × Area
= 1.3 × Area

(ii) Sowing of other crops like – bajra, mustard, moong, urad, moth, gram, peas, masoor and arhar (tur)

1 person × Area
= 0.1 x Area

3. Seeding rate

kcal/kg of seed x Amount of seed consumed (in kg.)
1 kcal = 0.00156 hp-hr

Total amount of seed (kcal) × 0.00156 hp-hr

Pre-determined norms for Tractor operated farms

1. Pre-harvest operations

– Tilling by manual and tractor involvement

1 person + fuel consumption
(in tractor) 21.99 hp-hrs

= (0.1 + 21.99) × Area × No. of tilling

= 22.09 × Area × No. of tilling

2. Sowing of crop

Sowing of wheat and barley
2 persons + fuel consumption
(in tractor) 21.99 hp-hrs***

= (0.2 + 21.99) x Area
= 22.19 × Area

Pre-determined norms for Tractor-bullock operated farms

I. Pre-harvest operations

In case of tractor and bullock operated farms, it is the tilling of land which is normally done with the help of tractors, casually hired on payment. Therefore, the multiple of energy equivalence will be same as in case of tractor operated farms. The remaining pre-harvest operations will be computed on the basis of same energy conversion equivalence as in case of bullock operated farms.

Pre-determined norms common to all bullock, tractor and tractor-bullock operated farms.

I. Pre-harvest operations

1. Weeding of crop

   1 hectare of land involves 2.468 hp-hrs****

2. Watering

   (i) Canal irrigation
   1 Person × Area
   = 0.1 × Area

   (ii) Tubewell irrigation
   1 Person + Electricity (Kwh = 1.34 hp-hrs) ×

*** As a tractor of 35 hp consumed 1.5 lit. of diesel as a fuel to work for an hour, therefore the energy equivalent of fuel consumed comes as :

1 lit. of diesel	=	9,400 kcal
1 hp	=	641 kcal
1 kcal	=	0.00156 hp-hr
Therefore 9,400 kcal	=	9,400 × 0.0015
Thus 1.5 litres diesel	=	14.66 × 1.5 = 21.99 hp-hrs

**** Hand weeding is a common practice and on an average 0.081 ha. of cropped land is weeded out by 2 persons (0.2 hp-hr) a day. As 1 hectare is equal to 12.34 *bighas* (a local hand measurement unit), its multiple will be 12.34 × 0.2 = 2.468 hp-hrs.

Area × No. of waterings

(iii) Irrigation by pumpset (diesel engine)

1 Person + fuel consumption
(in diesel engine) × Area × No. of waterings
= (0.1 + 21.99) × Area x No. of waterings
= 22.09 × Area × No. of waterings

3. Fertilizer consumption

(i) Nitrogenous 1 kg 14,325 kcal × 0.00156
= 22.347 hp-hrs

(ii) Phosphatic 1 kg 2,650 kcal × 0.00156
= 4.134 hp-hrs

(iii) Potassic 1 kg 1,600 kcal × 0.00156
= 2.496 hp-hrs

Fertilizer consumed (in kg) × Kcal × 0.0015 =

II. Post-harvest operations

1. Harvesting of crop

   (i) 1 hectare of cropped land is harvested by involving 3.702 hp-hrs

   (ii) 3.702 × Area

2. Drying of crop (other than potatoes and sugarcane)

   (i) 1 hectare of crop produce is looked after for sun drying by involving 4.936 hp-hrs

   (ii) 4.936 × Area

3. Thrashing of the crop produce (other than maize, wheat and barley crops)

   (a) Thrashing of other crops

   (i) Manual thrashing for 1 hectare crop produce involves 2.468 hp-hrs

   (ii) 2.468 × Area

(b) Thrashing of maize (including removal of corn cobs, transport and shelling (beating)

(i) Manual thrashing of 1 hectare of crop produce involves 4.196 hp-hrs

(ii) 4.195 × Area

(c) Thrashing of wheat and barley (by tractor-operated thrasher)

(i) 3 persons + fuel consumption (1.5 lit/hr) thrashes out 200 kg grains

[0.3 + 21.99]/200

= 0.111 hp/hr/100 kg

(ii) 0.111 × Total crop produce

Conversion of Output (crop produce) in Energy Equivalent

Specific values of grain crops and oilseeds were computed by considering the weightage of kcal to a kilogramme of grain crops and finally converted into horsepower-hr units by multiplying them with 0.00156 hp-hr. In case of sugarcane, the output was considered in terms of raw sugar which in extraction rate is one-fourth of the total sugarcane produced.

Energy Use and Crop Productivity in Aligarh District

For an in-depth analysis of energy use and crop productivity, the study considered 1135 farmers of 122 villages belonging to 17 development blocks of 6 tehsils of the Aligarh district. These farmers were designated on the basis of land-holdings as : marginal (with less than 1 hectare of land), small (1-2 hectares), semi-medium (2-4 hectares), medium (4-10 hectares) and large (with more than 10 hectares).

Considering the cultivated area devoted for growing the crops during *kharif* and *rabi* seasons, it was attempted to examine the crop output obtained and inputs applied by the farmers in pre-harvest and post-harvest phases of crop cultivation.

The farmers were further classified as those who are still operating their field with the bullocks for almost all the work needed during the pre-harvest and post-harvest phases. Such farms have been classified as : 'bullock operated farms'. The use of tractors in farming work has been well accepted by the farmers who can afford the expenses of work done by tractors in a speedy way. Tractors can either be owned by the farms or they can be hired for the work on payment basis. Those farmers who use tractor on farm for tilling the land, and transportation etc. were classed as : 'tractor operated farms'. Some farmers engage tractors to their farming for some specific purpose such as levelling and tilling of land, and therefore, some specific work is done by the tractor and for rest of the work, draught animals are needed. These farmers that engaged tractor and draught animals, were classed as : 'tractor-bullock operated farms'.

Inputs committed to crop by the farmers in pre-harvest operations include : the levelling and tilling of land (either by a pair of bullocks or tractor, and the repetition of tilling in numbers), sowing of seed, amount of seed needed (kg. per hectare), weeding and culture of crop (manually done and expressed in terms of man-hours/day), irrigation (through canal/tube-well/electric or diesel operated pumps; and number of water needed by the crop during its growth) and fertilization (type of fertilizer, doses with specific interval). The post-harvest phase of operations includes : harvesting, sun drying of produce (manually done and expressed in terms of man-hours/day), thrashing (by draught animal, manual and thrashers) and transportation of the thrashed output to the storage place.

Crop production (in kg.) of each category of farmer was first converted into kcal then into hp-hrs applying the conversion factors. As the crop output was converted into hp-hrs, the inputs were also converted into hp-hrs. While doing so, care was taken, that land preparation (bullocks/tractor operations) were given due consideration.

The investigations relating to use of energy for individual crop relates to cereal crops: wheat, rice, maize, barley and bajra (small millet); pulse crops; oilseeds; potatoes and sugarcane. For analysing the energy efficiency in crop production system wheat is selected as a type example. A sum of villages constituting a part of development block belonging to each tehsil of Aligarh district were selected for the establishment of input-output relation in wheat production. The detailed results of a comparative analysis of energy efficiency in wheat production of different farms in selected villages of blocks of each tehsil are shown in Appendices I to XI.

Energy efficiency analysis (as shown in Appendices I to XI) contains the number of bullock operated, tractor operated and tractor-bullock operated farms; number of farms belonging to marginal, small, semi-medium, medium and large categories of land-holdings representing all the three categories of farms (bullock, tractor and tractor-bullock operated farms); number of farmers surveyed; total and average area operated for the cultivation of wheat (in ha.); a sum total and average production (in kg.) of the crop; energy consumption (in hp-hrs) per operated farm during the pre-harvest operations in the form of : tilling of land, sowing seed, amount of seed consumed, weeding, watering and fertilization, and in post-harvest operations in the form of : harvesting of crop, sun drying of produce and thrashing. Finally at the end, the energy efficiency index is computed by dividing the sum total of crop production (in hp-hrs) to that of total energy consumption (in hp-hrs).

Tables 5.4 to 5.9 are an abstract form of Appendices I to XI and show the result of an input-output analysis of energy used in wheat production on some selected village farms of 6 development blocks as representatives of 6 tehsils in Aligarh district. It is seen from Table 5.4 that in the villages of Lodha block of Koil tehsil, the farmers belonging to marginal land holding category invested an average of 3030.87 hp-hrs per ha as an input for the cultivation of wheat, while they obtained an output of 5891.27 hp-hrs per ha achieving an efficiency index value of 1.94. Whereas, for the tractor operated farms, the average energy input was 3016.66 hp-hrs per hectare and the output obtained 7114.80 hp-hrs per ha and in terms of efficiency they are more efficient having an index value of 2.35. In case of tractor-bullock operated farms, the analysis indicates the input of 4460.84 hp-hrs per ha, and the output of 7341.18 hp-hrs per ha giving an index value of 1.64 as efficiency ratio.

Fig. 5.2 shows an input-output relationship for the farms belonging to marginal, small, semi-medium, medium and large land holding categories in individual villages as the representatives of the blocks and tehsils of Aligarh district.

Table 5.5 shows the input-output analysis of farms located in Iglas block of Iglas tehsil. It is seen from the table that, on bullock operated farms with marginal land-holdings, the farmers invested 5246.86 hp-hrs per ha in pre-harvest operations and 317.09 hp-hrs per ha on post-harvest operations. In terms of efficiency the index vlaue is 2.17. On the tractor operated farms with the marginal land-holding, the farmers invested 4228.00 hp-hrs per ha for pre-harvest operations and 181.88 hp-hrs per ha for post-havest operations giving an energy efficiency value of 1.94. On the marginal farms of tractor-bullock type of farming, there were 3927.48 hp-hrs per ha invested in pre-harvest operations and 179.32 hp-hrs per ha during post-harvest operations. This gives an energy efficiency index value of 3.63.

Fig. 5.3 shows a comparison of energy input-output in wheat production in some selected villages representing the concerned blocks and tehsils of Aligarh district.

Some results of the analysis of energy efficiency in wheat production on the selected farms of the villages of Mursan block in Hathras tehsil are shown in Table 5.6. On bullock operated farms with marginal land-holdings, farmers invested 5046.50 hp-hrs per ha in pre-harvest operations and 328.07 hp-hrs per ha in post-harvest operations achieving an energy efficiency index value of 1.88 whereas on tractor operated farms, the farmers with marginal land holding invested 3471.64 hp-hrs per ha on pre-harvest operations and 190.83 hp-hrs per ha on post-harvest operation giving an energy efficiency index value of 2.13. The tractor-bullock operated farms belonging to the marginal land-holdings provided 4692.87 hp-hrs per ha for pre-harvest operations and 541.19 hp-hrs per ha for post-harvest operation with a value of 1.85 as efficiency index.

Fig. 5.4 shows a comparison of input-output in wheat production on farms from some selected villages of respective blocks and tehsils of Aligarh district.

Similar results of comparative analysis of energy efficiency in wheat production obtained for the farms located in the blocks of Atrauli of Atrauli tehsil, Khair of Khair tehsil and Akrabad of Sikandra Rao tehsil are shown in Tables 5.7 to 5.9.

The results of energy input-output in wheat production shows that the district is efficient in terms of input-output ratio. The study may be helpful in raising the production of other crops in areas where the energy efficiency is slightly above the index value of 1 and to bring them to the level of areas which have the efficiency index equal to 2 or more than 2.

Table 5.4: Energy Input-Output in Wheat Production in Lodha Block of Koil Tehsil in Aligarh District

Type of farms	*Pre-harvest operations*	*Post-harvest operations*	*Total*	*Crop Energy Production (in hp-hrs)*	*Energy Efficiency Index*
I. Bullock operated					
1. Marginal	2906.04	124.83	3030.87	5891.27	1.94
2. Small	4564.66	251.97	4816.63	11895.73	2.46
3. Semi-medium	7976.19	467.24	8443.43	20384.98	2.41
4. Medium	28061.71	670.48	28731.48	37692.27	1.31
5. Large	Nil	Nil	Nil	Nil	Nil
II. Tractor operated					
1. Marginal	2866.28	150.38	3016.66	7114.80	2.35
2. Small	4302.19	434.41	4550.42	11717.86	2.57
3. Semi-medium	5734.56	340.59	6075.16	16072.98	2.64
4. Medium	11945.77	737.90	12683.67	34937.98	2.75
5. Large	17581.69	1218.59	18800.19	57780.80	3.07
III. Tractor-bullock operated					
1. Marginal	4304.16	156.68	4460.84	7314.18	1.64
2. Small	4397.99	251.54	4649.53	11841.83	2.54
3. Semi-medium	5476.45	357.24	5833.69	16924.60	2.90
4. Medium	14737.42	918.40	15655.82	43470.35	2.77
5. Large	Nil	Nil	Nil	Nil	Nil

Table 5.5: Energy Input-Output in Wheat Production in Iglas Block of Iglas Tehsil in Aligarh District

Type of farms	*Pre-harvest operations*	*Post-harvest operations*	*Total*	*Crop Energy Production (in hp-hrs)*	*Energy Efficiency Index*
I. Bullock operated					
1. Marginal	5246.86	317.09	5563.96	12127.50	2.17
2. Small	5631.49	276.95	5908.45	13221.67	2.23
3. Semi-medium	9985.51	627.09	10612.60	38781.05	3.65
4. Medium	Nil	Nil	Nil	Nil	Nil
5. Large	Nil	Nil	Nil	Nil	Nil
II. Tractor operated					
1. Marginal	4228.00	181.88	4409.88	8591.66	1.94
2. Small	3632.87	241.61	3874.48	11426.80	2.94
3. Semi-medium	10878.58	649.16	11527.75	30706.83	2.66
4. Medium	24330.81	1284.96	25615.78	60799.90	2.37
5. Large	Nil	Nil	Nil	Nil	Nil
III. Tractor-bullock operated					
1. Marginal	3927.48	179.32	4106.80	14934.19	3.63
2. Small	3946.24	212.75	4159.29	10025.40	2.41
3. Semi-medium	8708.28	477.86	9174.48	22638.00	2.46
4. Medium	14408.73	815.01	15222.25	38651.69	2.53
5. Large	27394.56	1699.58	29094.14	80488.87	2.76

Table 5.6: Energy Input-Output in Wheat Production in Mursan Block of Hathras Tehsil in Aligarh District

Type of farms	*Pre-harvest operations*	*Post-harvest operations*	*Total*	*Crop Energy Production (in hp-hrs)*	*Energy Efficiency Index*
I. Bullock operated					
1. Marginal	5046.50	328.07	5374.57	10133.20	1.88
2. Small	5520.37	185.29	5705.66	8624.00	1.51
3. Semi-medium	6977.19	429.76	7406.95	20352.64	2.74
4. Medium	Nil	Nil	Nil	Nil	Nil
5. Large	Nil	Nil	Nil	Nil	Nil
II. Tractor operated					
1. Marginal	4027.10	190.83	4217.93	9012.08	2.13
2. Small	4119.39	210.30	4329.69	9863.70	2.27
3. Semi-medium	8526.61	425.04	8951.65	19943.00	2.22
4. Medium	15564.73	686.99	16251.73	32340.00	1.98
5. Large	Nil	Nil	Nil	Nil	Nil
III. Tractor-bullock operated					
1. Marginal	10506.59	541.19	11047.79	20482.00	1.85
2. Small	5655.69	231.45	5887.14	10780.00	1.83
3. Semi-medium	6355.55	508.42	6863.97	24147.50	3.51
4. Medium	Nil	Nil	Nil	Nil	Nil
5. Large	Nil	Nil	Nil	Nil	Nil

Table 5.7: Energy Input-Output in Wheat Production in Atrauli Block of Atrauli Tehsil in Aligarh District

Type of farms	*Pre-harvest operations*	*Post-harvest operations*	*Total*	*Crop Energy Production (in hp-hrs)*	*Energy Efficiency Index*
I. Bullock operated					
1. Marginal	4990.74	161.17	5151.91	7546.00	1.46
2. Small	3405.44	272.41	3677.86	12936.00	3.51
3. Semi-medium	5486.20	415.83	5902.03	19704.84	3.33
4. Medium	11192.76	752.75	12031.23	34954.15	2.90
5. Large	Nil	Nil	Nil	Nil	Nil
II. Tractor operated					
1. Marginal	Nil	Nil	Nil	Nil	Nil
2. Small	6008.03	543.25	6551.29	20482.00	3.12
3. Semi-medium	7787.25	483.69	8270.94	22853.60	2.76
4. Medium	9343.80	579.49	9923.30	27435.10	2.76
5. Large	Nil	Nil	Nil	Nil	Nil
III. Tractor-bullock operated					
1. Marginal	5127.07	362.19	5489.26	11858.00	2.16
2. Small	6706.05	390.64	7096.70	18487.70	2.60
3. Semi-medium	8165.01	436.35	8601.36	21991.20	2.55
4. Medium	Nil	Nil	Nil	Nil	Nil
5. Large	Nil	Nil	Nil	Nil	Nil

Table 5.8: Energy Input-Output in Wheat Production in Khair Block of Khair Tehsil in Aligarh District

Type of farms	*Pre-harvest operations*	*Post-harvest operations*	*Total*	*Crop Energy Production (in hp-hrs)*	*Energy Efficiency Index*
I. Bullock operated					
1. Marginal	3551.05	249.79	3800.85	8624.00	2.26
2. Small	7372.33	401.15	7773.48	18918.90	2.43
3. Semi-medium	9591.01	449.20	10025.93	23392.60	2.33
4. Medium	13599.08	803.55	14402.64	37789.29	2.62
5. Large	Nil	Nil	Nil	Nil	Nil
II. Tractor operated					
1. Marginal	2966.87	98.08	3064.96	4635.40	1.51
2. Small	4787.79	262.92	5037.38	12359.27	2.45
3. Semi-medium	9756.48	451.24	10207.73	22853.60	2.23
4. Medium	23830.24	1257.13	25087.38	59290.00	2.36
5. Large	31690.45	1373.98	33064.43	64680.00	1.95
III. Tractor-bullock operated					
1. Marginal	3981.62	213.49	4195.12	9163.00	2.18
2. Small	6072.81	314.87	6387.68	14822.50	2.32
3. Semi-medium	6131.74	701.04	6832.80	14358.96	2.10
4. Medium	11285.41	845.11	12130.52	40317.20	3.32
5. Large	Nil	Nil	Nil	Nil	Nil

Table 5.9: Energy Input-Output in Wheat Production in Akrabad Block of Sikandra Rao Tehsil in Aligarh District

Type of farms	*Pre-harvest operations*	*Post-harvest operations*	*Total*	*Crop Energy Production (in hp-hrs)*	*Energy Efficiency Index*
I. Bullock operated					
1. Marginal	3342.80	165.64	3508.45	7793.94	2.22
2. Small	4712.85	311.90	5024.75	14784.77	2.94
3. Semi-medium	6618.01	423.51	7041.53	21931.91	3.11
4. Medium	40977.52	1869.98	42847.50	88935.00	2.07
5. Large	Nil	Nil	Nil	Nil	Nil
II. Tractor operated					
1. Marginal	2815.15	118.06	2933.21	5551.70	1.89
2. Small	3728.60	245.16	3973.34	11577.72	2.91
3. Semi-medium	5786.63	424.48	6211.11	17064.74	2.74
4. Medium	15464.17	951.01	16415.18	45006.50	2.74
5. Large	14361.93	1563.53	15925.46	74403.56	4.67
III. Tractor-bullock operated					
1. Marginal	5125.75	362.19	5487.95	10241.00	1.86
2. Small	6704.31	390.64	7094.95	18487.70	2.60
3. Semi-medium	8162.61	436.35	8598.96	21991.20	2.55
4. Medium	Nil	Nil	Nil	Nil	Nil
5. Large	Nil	Nil	Nil	Nil	Nil

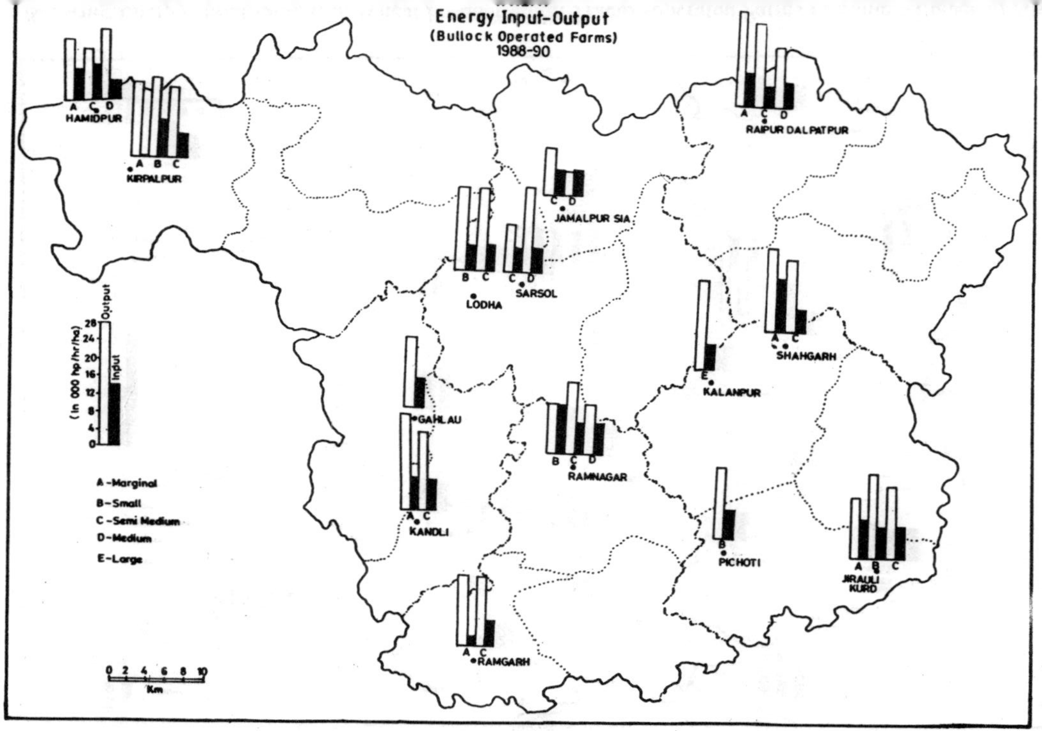

Fig. 5.2: Showing Energy Input-Output in Wheat Production on Bullock-operated Farms in Some Villages of Aligarh District

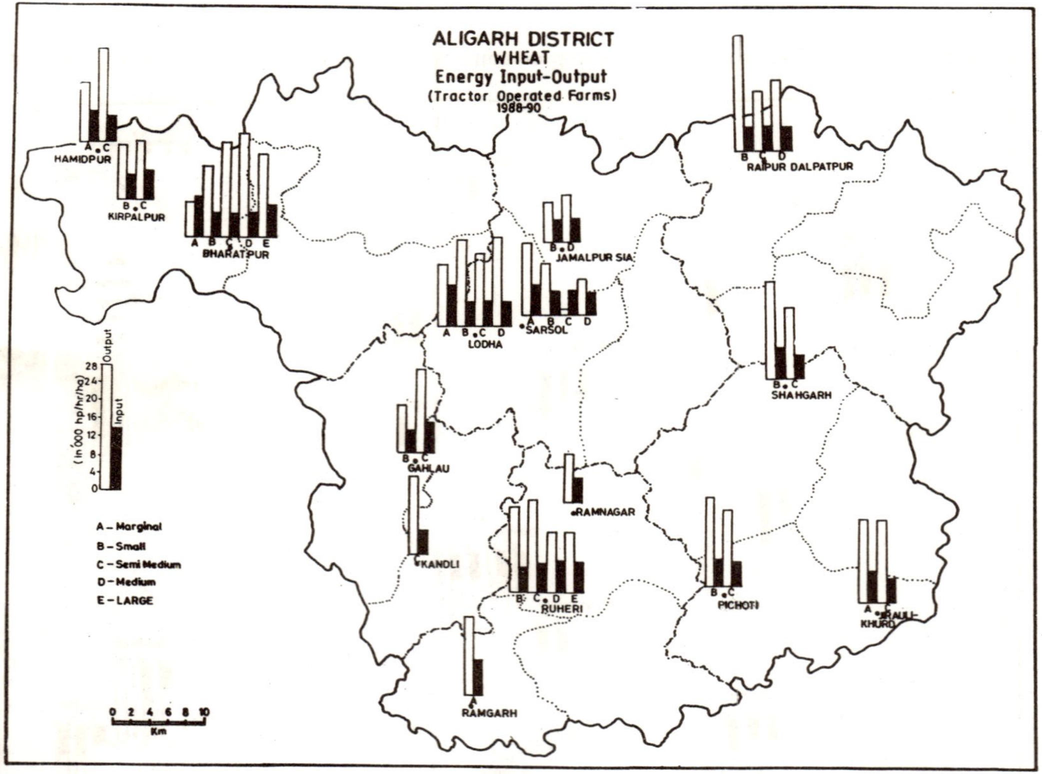

Fig 5.3: Showing Energy Input-Output in Wheat Production on Tractor-operated Farms in Some Villages of Aligarh District

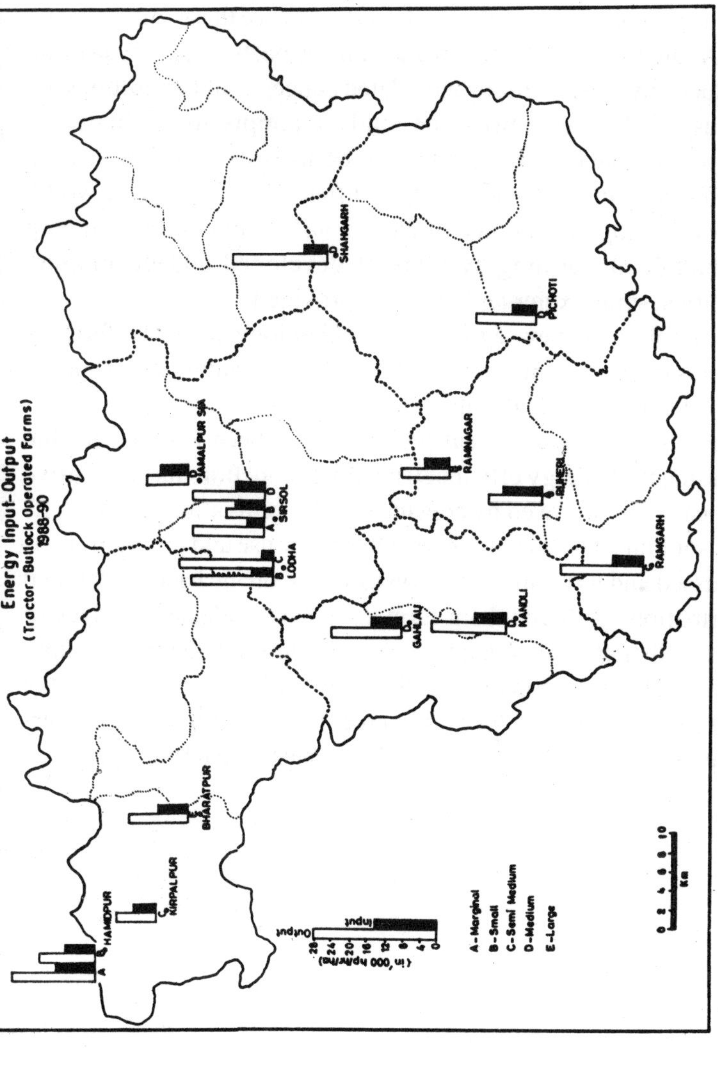

Fig. 5.4: Showing Energy Input-Output in Wheat Production on Tractor-bullock-operated Farms in Some Villages of Aligarh District

CONCLUSION

In a country where cultivation of crops is the mainstay of population, assessment of energy use in agriculture and measurement of productivity in a region is of great significance. It will help in locating imbalances and suggest the methods to remove these imbalances.

At the first place in this work, some aspects of energy use and productivity in agriculture and related concepts and definitions are discussed. Subsequently, the study attempts to evaluate the approaches that have been made for the analysis of energy use and measurement of crop productivity in different countries of the world. For examining the contrast of energy inflow and outflow in crop production in farming systems of developed and developing countries, some examples have been provided.

Adoption of new agricultural technology in many farming systems in developing countries has made cultivation more energy intensive particularly during the phase of green revolution.

Finally, methodological procedure has been evolved for the assessment of energy efficiency in crop production. Its elaborative application is followed by considering the cultivation of wheat, its input-output analysis with respect to energy use and productivity is discussed and its relationship is established on the basis of detailed informations gathered from farmers in some selected villages of Aligarh district. The variations emerging out from the input-output analysis of wheat crop reveals, that they are the result partly of the farm practices (experience and perception) of individual farmers and partly are due to the resources available to the farmers involved in the cultivation of crop.

APPENDICES

APPENDIX I

GEOGRAPHERS' OPINION ON AGRICULTURAL PRODUCTIVITY

A.N. Rakitnikov : Geographical Faculty, Moscow University, U.S.S.R.

A. Methods of measuring intensity of agriculture having necessary basic data: (a) value of fixed and floating assets, i.e., total of production inputs per unit area of agricultural land, (b) this most general quantitative index should be supplemented by separate calculations of value of production funds/reserves/per unit area and labour input in hours or days per unit area, and (c) as a supplementary index a value of gross production of agriculture per unit area should also be applied.

B. To determine land productivity either partial indices/yields of particular crops, value of gross crop production or general quantitative expressions value of total final production could be used. The same to determine labour productivity in agriculture in relation to working hours or days. To determine economic effectiveness of capital inputs/ productivity of capital inputs, a value of final production of value of fixed and floating assets should be related.

J.E. Spencer : Department of Geography, University of California, Los Angeles, U.S.A.

Intensity of agriculture, I understand to be an index of how much of the year the crop surface, be it soil or water in a pond, is occupied by crops, in a ratio of how many crops are grown per year, measured normally against some kind of productivity factor. The latter could be calories or it could be dollars.

J.J.A. Taylor and J.W. Aitchison : Department of Geography University College of Wales, Aberystwyth, U.K.

A. Intensity of production should ideally be measured by total monetary input with allowances for the work of the entrepreneur and his family plus interest on his invest capital. This again would be difficult to apply and partial measures might have to suffice, e.g., yields, stock densities, total grain units, or labour inputs per unit area. A slightly equivocal method would be gross output per unit area; high outputs usually intimate high inputs.

B. Land, labour and capital productivity are partial measures of agricultural productivity. They are extremely difficult to measure independently because they are complementary rather than isolated aspects. Thus, a measure of land productivity, e.g. output per acre would not necessarily be an indicator of land potential, but rather a measure of the combined utilization of land, labour and capital. In the same way, labour productivity, e.g., output per man day is as much a reflection of innate land potential and the degree of capital investment as it is of labour efficiency. In the final economic analysis land and labour reduced into the debit side of the farm account and ultimately affect capital productivity. The later is the same, as agricultural productivity, i.e., output per unit of input in monetary terms.

B. Hofmeister : Institute of Geography, Technical University, West Berlin

A. Intensity of agriculture refers to inputs of manpower, technical equipment and materials, such as seeds and fertilizers per unit area.

B. In order to measure land, labour and capital productivity of agriculture net yields/value/per unit area, per man power unit, and as a percentage of total capital investment.

L.Reed: Department of Geography, McMaster University, Hamilton, Ontario, Canada.

The best measure of the intensity of agriculture is to ascertain expenditures on capital and labour per unit area of farm land. This information is not readily available in complete form from the census. Total capitalization and number of full time farmers per unit area is available and thus it is the most satisfactory index to be used in Canada. Another good indicator of intensity is the percentage of cultivated crop land per unit area.

H. Shirahama : Chiba University, Chiba, Japan

We do not have the overall statistics wich are adequate to measure labour or capital productivity of agriculture in Japan. There is no choice then but to estimate the productivity from samples of individual farm management. Land productivity may be measured by the gross/monetary production per acreage of cultivated land per area.

APPENDIX II

QUESTIONNAIRE SCHEDULE FOR CONDUCTING VILLAGE LEVEL SURVEY FOR THE ANALYSIS OF ENERGY EFFICIENCY IN FOOD PRODUCTION SYSTEM AT DEVELOPMENT BLOCK/TEHSIL/DISTRICT

1. General Information

Date.................
Name of the Village
Name of the Development Block
Name of the Tehsil

1. General land use

(i) Gross cultivated area (in ha.)..
(ii) Net cultivated area in the Kharif season (in ha.)...........
(iii) Net cultivated area in the Rabi season (in ha.)...............
(iv) Double cropped area (in ha.)...
Name of the farmer.................... s/o...........................
Address Street/Village...
Family members with age and educational qualifications:

	No.	*Age*	*Educational Qualification*
(i) Male.......			
(ii) Female............			
(iii) Children...........			

2. Landholding

(i) Size of farm (in ha.)
(ii) Owned............. (Irrigated..............rainfed...........)
(iii) Hired............... (Irrigated............rainfed...........)

3. ***Type of farming***
   (i) Tractor-operated
   (ii) Bullock-operated
   (iii) Tractor-bullock operated

4. ***Human energy used***

	No.	Age
(i) Farm labour (casually hired)		
(ii) Farm labour (family member)		

5. ***Source of irrigation*** — Area irrigated (in ha.)
   (i) Canal
   (ii) Tubewell
   (iii) Well
   (iv) Other sources

6. ***Agricultural equipment, implement and machinery in operation***

   Item — No.
   (i) Manually operated.................................
   (ii) Bullock operated.....................................
   (iii) Power operated (model with hp.) ....
   (iv) Self-propelled..
   (a) Tractor (model with hp.) ....
   (b) Diesel engine/pumpset..............................
   (c) Electric motor/pumpset............................

II. *7.* ***Energy used***

	Man	Bullock	Mechanical/Tractor(hp.)
Land preparation	......	....	....
Tilling	......	....	....
Sowing	......	....	....
Weeding	......	....	....

8. Cropping Pattern and Crop Production/Yield

Season/ Crop	Area (in ha.)	Seed variety	Seed rate (kg/ha)	Production (in qnts.)	Yield (qnts./ ha.)	Remarks
Kharif Crops						
Rice						
Jowar						
Bajra						
Maize						
Urd						
Moong						
Moth						
Sugarcane						
Rabi Crops						
Wheat						
Barley						
Gram						
Peas						
Groundnut						
Mustard						
Rapeseed						
Til						
Potato						

9. Fertilizers Used

	Type of fertilizer			Farmyard manure	Other manures
	Urea	SSP	Murate of potash		
Kharif Crops Quantity used.............					
Rabi Crops Quantity used............					

10. Petroleum/diesel/mobil oil consumed in crop production (in liters)

(i) In tractor

(ii) In diesel engine

11. Irrigation by Tubewell

(i) Tube well no. of hours run ....

(ii) Electricity bill paid for irrigation in (average of 12 months) Rs.............

12. Energy used in Post-harvest operations

(i) Manual

(ii) Bullock

(iii) Tractor

(iv) Thrashing and winnowing

13. Energy Requirement for Crop produce, and Transportation from Farm to home/store

(i) Transportation from farm to home/store

Season/ Crop	*Quantity (in qnts.)*	*Mode of transportation*	*Distance (one way) km.*	*Man-hours spent*				*Other sources of energy used*
				Loading	*Unloading*	*Transportation*	*Weighing*	
Kharif Crops								
Rice								
Jowar								
Bajra								
Maize								
Urd								
Moong								
Moth								
Sugarcane								
Rabi Crops								
Wheat								
Barley								
Gram								
Peas								
Groundnut								
Mustard								
Rapeseed								
Til								
Potato								

(ii) Transportation of crop produce to market

Season/ Crop	Quantity (in qnts.)	Mode of transportation	Distance (one way) km.	Man-hours spent				Other sources of energy used
				Loading	Unloading	Transportation	Weighing	
Kharif Crops								
Rice								
Jowar								
Bajra								
Maize								
Urd								
Moong								
Moth								
Sugarcane								
Rabi Crops								
Wheat								
Barley								
Gram								
Peas								
Groundnut								
Mustard								
Rapeseed								
Til								
Potato								

14. Energy Required for Drying and Storage of Crop Produce

Season/ Crop	*Quan-tity*	*Energy used*				*Remarks*
		Drying		*Storage*		
		Labour	*Time (hrs)*	*Labour*	*Time (hrs)*	
Kharif Crops						
Rice						
Jowar						
Bajra						
Maize						
Urd						
Moong						
Moth						
Sugarcane						
Rabi Crops						
Wheat						
Barley						
Gram						
Peas						
Groundnut						
Mustard						
Rapeseed						
Til						
Potato						

15. Method of storage

	Kharif produce (in kg/qnts.)	Rabi produce (in kg/qnts.)	Total quantity (in kg/qnts
(i) In metal bins			
(ii) In bags			
(iii) In earthen pots			

16. Energy Required for Crop Processing (milling, hulling, etc.)

Season/ Crop	*Quantity processed (in qnts.)*	*Type of proce-ssing*	*Crop/ grain transport (man-hrs or other sources of energy used)*	*Energy requirement processing*		*Remarks*
				Man-hrs.	*Others (mech./ elect.)*	
Kharif Crops						
Rice						
Jowar						
Bajra						
Maize						
Urd						
Moong						
Moth						
Sugarcane						
Rabi Crops						
Wheat						
Barley						
Gram						
Peas						
Groundnut						
Mustard						
Rapeseed						
Til						
Potato						

APPENDIX III

NUMBER OF FARMERS APPROACHED FOR CONDUCTING THE SURVEYS IN ALIGARH DISTRICT

Tehsil	*Block*	*Village*	*No. of farmers interrograted*
1	2	3	4
Atrauli	**Atrauli**	Jamalgarhi	11
		Malahpur	12
		Narauna Aqapur	10
		Raipur- Dalpatpur	10
	Total	**4**	**43**
	Bijoli	Haibatpur	10
		Rustamnagar	9
	Total	**2**	**17**
	Charra	Barla	8
		Bhamori Buzurg	9
		Nausha	10
	Total	**3**	**29**
	Gangiri	Chabilpur	9
		Charra	8
		Datawali	9
		Dhansari	8
		Rukhala	9
		Tikta	8
	Total	**6**	**51**
Hathras	**Hathras**	Ahan	10
		Bahanpur	8
		Gijrauli	8
		Jafarabad	9
		Mirzapur	10
		Nagla Imliya	8
		Pura Kalan	8

1	2	3	4
	Total	**7**	**61**
	Mursan	Chitabar	10
		Mahmoodpur-Brahmanan	9
		Ramgarh	7
	Total	**3**	**26**
	Sasni	Lutsan	5
		Ramnagar	8
		Ruheri	9
	Total	**3**	**22**
Iglas	**Iglas**	Bahanpur	10
		Kajrauth	8
		Kandli	10
		Mahua	10
		Nagla Frahar	5
		Naya Bans	11
		Sahara Kalan	11
		Taharpur	12
		Udaipur	12
	Total	**9**	**89**
	Gonda	Gahlau	10
		Nagla Jhujar	11
	Total	**2**	21
Khair	**Khair**	Andla	10
		Gaumat	9
		Manpur Khurd	10
		Narayanpur	10
		Nayabans	8
		Sangrampur	10
		Sujanpur	10
	Total	**7**	**67**
	Chandaus	Chuharpur	7
		Gabhana	4
		Pahawati	10

1	2	3	4
		Palla Sallu	10
		Somna	8
	Total	**5**	**39**
	Tappal	Bharatpur	10
		Hamidpur	13
		Kirpalpur	14
		Kurna	9
	Total	**4**	**46**
Koil	**Dhanipur**	Adon	6
		Alehdadpur	7
		Barotha	13
		Bhojpur	10
		Dhanipur	6
		Morthal	15
		Nagla Ausaf Ali	7
		Panethi	8
		Safedpura	6
		Sindhauli	17
	Total	**10**	**95**
	Jawan	Bajgarhi	8
		Jamalpur Sia	10
		Jungalgarhi	8
		Jawan- Sikandarpur	8
		Khushalgarhi	5
		Manzoorgarhi	4
		Satha	8
		Tejpur	9
	Total	**8**	**60**
	Lodha	Akbarpur	8
		Bajeedpur	10
		Bhartari	12
		Chilkora	12
		Digsi	10
		Elampur	11
		Hardaspur	9
		Karsua	9

1	2	3	4
		Kawarsi	10
		Kothia	11
		Lodha	14
		Madar Khera	2
		Mahua Khera	8
		Mehrawal	4
		Mukandpur	10
		Noorpur	14
		Pariyawali	10
		Pala Asia	9
		Sarsol	17
		Shahpur Qutub	11
		Talaspur Kalan	9
	Total	**21**	**210**
Sikandra Rao	**Akrabad**	Baroth	12
		Chandpur Mirzapur	10
		Gopi	12
		Kalanpur	4
		Ladhaua	11
		Mandanpur	20
		Nagaria Patti Chaharam	15
		Nagla Sartaja	8
		Pilakhna	10
		Qasimpur	14
		Shahgarh	9
		Sikandarpur	8
	Total	**12**	**133**
	Hasayan	Baramai	12
		Jirauli Khurd	8
		Purdil Nagar	8
		Rati Ka Nagla	9
	Total	**4**	**37**
	Sikandra Rao	Agsoli	7
		Bajidpur (Leha)	7
		Bartar Khas	6
		Dhansari	5

1	2	3	4
		Iqbalpur	6
		Mahamai Salabatnagar	8
		Mahmoodpur (Nagla Dhak)	9
		Nagla Chikna	8
		Nagla Jalal	10
		Pachaita	7
		Pichhoti	8
		Raipur Tappa Paura	10
	Total	**12**	**91**
	Grand Total	**122**	**1137**

APPENDIX IV

GENERAL INFORMATION

1.	General Information	Name of village, block and tahsil to which the village belong
2.	General Land Use of the Village	
3.	Farmer's Family Status	No. of persons: males, females and children and educational qualification
4.	Size of Land Holding (in ha.)	Ownership of land, (or of land) leased : in/out
5.	Type of Farming	Bullock, tractor or tractor-bullock operated farm
6.	Human Labour	Nos. used for various farm works
7.	Sources of Irrigation	Canal tube-well, pump set diesel/electric
8.	Agricultural Equipment, Implement and Machinery in Operation	Manually operated, bullock or power operated
9.	Cropping Pattern and Yield of Crops	Land under specific crop and energy used in kharif and rabi seasons; yield/ production of crop
10.	Consumption of Fertility (Quantity kg/ha)	Type of chemical fertilizers-urea, single super phosphate (SSP), potassic and DAP
11.	Consumption of Farmyard Manure	Quantity per hectare
12.	Fuel Consumption	Petrol/diesel/mobil oil consumed in tractor pumping set and threshing machine

13.	Energy used for Irrigation	No. of hours run per pumping set/tube-well
14.	Energy used for Post-harvest Operations	Harvesting and threshing–energy contributed by animate and mechanical sources
15.	Energy Used for Crop Drying and Keeping in Storage	Manual/animal
16.	Energy Used for Transportation of Crop Produce from Farm to Home/Storage Ground	Mode of transportation, distance covered, mandays—hours spent on loading, transportation, unloading and weighing the produce
17.	Energy Used for Transportation of Crop Produce from home/ Storage to Market	Mode of transportation, distance covered, mandays hours spent on loading, transportation, unloading and weighing the produce
18.	Energy used for Crop Produce Processing	

APPENDIX V

CROPPING PATTERN, ENERGY USED AND CROP PRODUCTION OF THE FARM IN A VILLAGE IN ALIGARH DISTRICT

Season/ Crop	Inputs							Output	
	Area (in ha.)	*Tilling of land (in ha.)*	*Sowing of seed*	*Seed rate (in kg.)*	*Weeding (in no.)*	*Fertilizer consumption (in kg.)*	*Watering (in no.)*	*Yielding (in kg./ha.)*	*Total production (in kg.)*
Kharif crop									
1									
2									
Rabi crop									
1									
2									

APPENDIX VI

A COMPARATIVE ANALYSIS OF ENERGY EFFICIENCY IN WHEAT PRODUCTION OF DIFFERENT FARMS IN SELECTED VILLAGES OF LODHA BLOCK OF KOIL TAHSIL IN ALIGARH DISTRICT

Item	*Bullock Operated Farms*				
	Marginal	*Small*	*Semi-medium*	*Medium*	*Large*
No. of farms surveyed	6	22	31	11	Nil
Total area operated (in ha)	2.41	17.71	42.68	26.31	
Average area per operated farm (in ha)	0.40	0.80	1.37	2.39	
Total crop production (in kg)	6,560	48,560	117,240	76,920	Nil
Average production per operated farm (in kg)	1,093	2,207	3,782	6,993	
A. Energy consumption per operated farm (in HP)					
I. Pre-harvest operations					
1. Tilling of land	2.31	4.80	9.45	17.74	
2. Sowing of seed	0.52	1.04	10.21	3.10	
3. Seed consumed	290.12	596.67	877.29	1627.98	
4. Weeding	0.99	0.13	0.81	0.81	
5. Watering	4.94	5.56	56.07	57.86	
6. Fertilizer	2607.15	3956.43	7022.36	10340.56	
Sub-total	2906.04	4564.66	7976.19	28061.71	Nil
II. Post-harvest operations					
1. Harvesting	1.49	2.99	29.07	8.85	
2. Drying of produce	1.98	3.97	38.79	11.80	
3. Threshing	121.36	245.00	399.24	649.83	
Sub-total	124.83	251.97	467.24	670.48	Nil
Grand Total (I + II)	3030.87	4816.63	8443.43	28731.48	Nil
B. Crop Production (in HP)	5891.27	11895.73	20384.98	27692.27	
C. Energy Consumption (in HP)	3030.87	4816.63	8443.43	28731.48	
Energy Efficiency Index	1.94	2.46	2.41	1.31	

Appendix-VI (*Contd.*)

Item	*Tractor Operated Farms*				
	Marginal	*Small*	*Semi-medium*	*Medium*	*Large*
No. of farms surveyed	17	14	22	18	3
Total area operated (in ha)	7.89	11.15	24.50	38.77	9.91
Average area per operated farm (in ha)	0.46	0.79	1.11	2.15	3.31
Total crop production (in kg)	22,440	30,440	65,600	116,685	32,160
Average production per operated farm (in kg)	1,320	2,174	2,982	6,482	10,720
A. Energy consumption per operated farm (in HP)					
I. Pre-harvest operations					
1. Tilling of land	50.22	87.191	129.54	326.48	572.83
2. Sowing of seed	10.31	21.24	24.69	36.41	73.42
3. Seed consumed	333.44	562.89	809.39	1445.05	2302.97
4. Weeding	0.73	0.52	0.23	0.82	—
5. Watering	13.41	10.50	21.96	15.62	24.98
6. Fertilizer	2458.17	3623.40	4748.73	10109.69	14607.49
Sub-total	2866.28	4302.19	5734.56	11945.77	17581.69
II. Post-harvest operations					
1. Harvesting	1.72	2.94	4.12	7.92	12.25
2. Drying of produce	2.29	3.90	5.47	10.52	16.33
3. Threshing	146.37	241.34	331.00	719.44	1189.92
Sub-total	150.38	434.41	340.59	737.90	1218.50
Grand Total (I + II)	3016.66	4550.42	6075.16	12683.67	18800.19
B. Crop Production (in HP)	7114.80	11717.86	16072.98	34937.98	57780.80
C. Energy Consumption (in HP)	3016.66	4550.42	6075.16	12683.67	18800.19
Energy Efficiency Index	2.35	2.57	2.64	2.75	3.07

Appendix-VI (*Contd.*)

Item	Tractor-bullock Operated Farms				
	Marginal	*Small*	*Semi-medium*	*Medium*	*Large*
No. of farms surveyed	8	13	13	11	Nil
Total area operated (in ha)	5.04	11.64	13.08	29.47	
Average area per operated farm (in ha)	0.63	0.89	1.00	2.67	
Total crop production (in kg)	10,900	28,560	40,820	88,720	Nil
Average production per operated farm (in kg)	1,362	2,197	3,140	8,065	
A. Energy consumption per operated farm (in HP)					
I. Pre-harvest operations					
1. Tilling of land	107.15	102.03	144.41	348.20	
2. Sowing of seed	1.51	1.97	2.23	2.13	
3. Seed consumed	448.00	573.80	729.09	1905.84	
4. Weeding	0.66	0.21	0.37	1.29	
5. Watering	4.45	6.05	7.16	20.20	
6. Fertilizer	3742.37	3867.75	4593.16	12439.76	
Sub-total	4304.16	4397.99	5476.45	14737.42	Nil
II. Post-harvest operations					
1. Harvesting	2.33	3.29	3.72	9.91	
2. Drying of produce	3.11	4.39	4.96	13.22	
3. Threshing	151.23	243.85	348.54	895.26	
Sub-total	156.68	251.54	357.24	918.40	Nil
Grand Total (I + II)	4460.84	4649.53	5833.69	15655.82	Nil
B. Crop Production (in HP)	7341.18	11841.83	16924.60	43470.35	
C. Energy Consumption (in HP)	4460.84	4649.53	5833.69	15655.82	
Energy Efficiency Index	1.64	2.54	2.90	2.77	

APPENDIX VII

A COMPARATIVE ANALYSIS OF ENERGY EFFICIENCY IN WHEAT PRODUCTION OF DIFFERENT FARMS IN SELECTED VILLAGES OF IGLAS BLOCK OF IGLAS TAHSIL IN ALIGARH DISTRICT

	Bullock Operated Farms				
Item	*Marginal*	*Small*	*Semi-medium*	*Medium*	*Large*
No. of farms surveyed	2	2	27	Nil	Nil
Total area operated (in ha)	1.45	2.75	48.44		
Average area per operated farm (in ha)	0.72	0.91	1.79		
Total crop production (in kg)	4,500	7,.360	194,280	Nil	Nil
Average production per operated farm (in kg)	2,250	2,453	7,195		
A. Energy consumption per operated farm (in HP)					
I. Pre-harvest operations					
1. Tilling of land	6.32	6.32	19.71		
2. Sowing of seed	0.94	1.19	2.64		
3. Seed consumed	539.76	651.31	1456.01		
4. Weeding	0.99	1.73	2.52		
5. Watering	5.96	54.90	92.22		
6. Fertilizer	4992.87	4916.34	8412.40		
Sub-total	5246.86	5631.49	9985.51	Nil	Nil
II. Post-harvest operations					
1. Harvesting	2.69	3.39	7.50		
2. Drying of produce	3.59	1.23	10.00		
3. Threshing	310.80	272.32	609.59		
Sub-total	317.09	276.95	627.09	Nil	Nil
Grand Total (I + II)	5563.96	5908.45	10612.60	Nil	Nil
B. Crop Production (in HP)	12127.50	13221.67	38781.05		
C. Energy Consumption (in HP)	5563.96	5908.45	10612.60		
Energy Efficiency Index	2.17	2.23	3.65		

Appendix-VII (*Contd.*)

Item	*Tractor Operated Farms*				
	Marginal	*Small*	*Semi-medium*	*Medium*	*Large*
No. of farms surveyed	10	4	9	9	Nil
Total area operated (in ha)	5.73	2.91	16.60	34.26	
Average area per operated farm (in ha)	0.57	0.72	1.84	3.80	
Total crop production (in kg)	15,940	8,480	51,280	101,520	Nil
Average production per operated farm (in kg)	1,594	2,120	5,697	11,280	
A. Energy consumption per operated farm (in HP)					
I. Pre-harvest operations					
1. Tilling of land	74.01	61.28	301.313	903.53	
2. Sowing of seed	12.71	16.17	40.94	84.48	
3. Seed consumed	426.95	501.97	1481.94	2956.68	
4. Weeding	1.39	1.04	2.84	4.66	
5. Watering	52.49	35.53	192.196	368.45	
6. Fertilizer	3660.43	3016.84	8859.34	20012.98	
Sub-total	4228.00	3632.87	10878.58	24330.81	Nil
II. Post-harvest operations					
1. Harvesting	2.12	2.69	7.60	14.09	
2. Drying of produce	2.82	3.59	9.10	18.79	
3. Threshing	176.93	235.32	632.45	1252.08	
Sub-total	181.88	241.61	649.16	1284.96	Nil
Grand Total (I + II)	4409.88	3874.48	11527.75	25615.78	Nil
B. Crop Production (in HP)	8591.66	11426.80	30706.83	60799.20	
C. Energy Consumption (in HP)	4409.88	3874.48	11527.75	25615.78	
Energy Efficiency Index	1.94	2.94	2.66	2.37	

Appendix-VII (*Contd.*)

Item	*Tractor-bullock Operated Farms*				
	Marginal	*Small*	*Semi-medium*	*Medium*	*Large*
No. of farms surveyed	7	4	3	7	3
Total area operated (in ha)	3.96	2.91	4.06	15.39	14.58
Average area per operated farm (in ha)	0.56	0.72	1.35	2.19	4.86
Total crop production (in kg)	11,000	7,440	12,600	50,200	44,800
Average production per operated farm (in kg)	1,571	1,860	4,200	7,171	14,933
A. Energy consumption per operated farm (in HP)					
I. Pre-harvest operations					
1. Tilling of land	76.17	75.15	213.521	544.48	1002.00
2. Sowing of seed	1.36	0.58	2.99	1.75	3.88
3. Seed consumed	467.27	566.74	899.60	1603.85	3490.44
4. Weeding	0.68	1.69	1.33	3.42	2.66
5. Watering	29.93	6.17	67.34	124.01	176.13
6. Fertilizer	3352.05	3296.18	7523.49	12131.22	22719.45
Sub-total	3927.48	3946.54	8708.28	14408.73	27394.56
II. Post-harvest operations					
1. Harvesting	2.09	2.69	4.99	8.13	17.99
2. Drying of produce	2.79	3.59	4.66	10.85	23.99
3. Threshing	174.42	206.46	466.200	796.02	1457.60
Sub-total	179.32	212.75	477.86	815.01	1699.58
Grand Total (I + II)	4106.80	4159.29	9174.48	15222.25	29094.14
B. Crop Production (in HP)	14934.19	10025.40	22638.00	38651.69	80488.87
C. Energy Consumption (in HP)	4106.80	4159.29	9174.48	15222.25	29034.14
Energy Efficiency Index	3.63	2.41	2.46	2.53	2.76

APPENDIX VIII

A COMPARATIVE ANALYSIS OF ENERGY EFFICIENCY IN WHEAT PRODUCTION OF DIFFERENT FARMS IN SELECTED VILLAGES OF MURSAN BLOCK OF HATHRAS TAHSIL IN ALIGARH DISTRICT

Item	*Bullock Operated Farms*				
	Marginal	*Small*	*Semi-medium*	*Medium*	*Large*
No. of farms surveyed	1	1	5	Nil	Nil
Total area operated (in ha)	0.97	0.89	6.15		
Average area per operated farm (in ha)	0.97	0.89	1.23		
Total crop production (in kg)	1,880	1,600	3,776		
Average production per operated farm (in kg)	1,880	1,600	3,776		
A. Energy consumption per operated farm (in HP)					
I. Pre-harvest operations					
1. Tilling of land	5.34	6.86	10.97		
2. Sowing of seed	0.77	0.71	0.98		
3. Seed consumed	906.79	593.73	984.62		
4. Weeding	2.39	2.19	3.30		
5. Watering	107.35	0.53	77.99		
6. Fertilizer	4023.86	4916.34	5899.60		
Sub-total	5046.50	5520.37	6977.19	Nil	N il
II. Post-harvest operations					
1. Harvesting	3.59	3.29	4.55		
2. Drying of produce	4.79	4.39	6.07		
3. Threshing	319.68	177.60	419.13		
Sub-total	328.07	185.29	429.76	Nil	Nil
Grand Total (I + II)	5374.57	5705.66	7406.95	Nil	Nil
B. Crop Production (in HP)	10133.20	8624.00	20352.64		
C. Energy Consumption (in HP)	5375.22	5705.66	7406.95		
Energy Efficiency Index	1.88	1.51	2.74		

Appendix-VIII (*Contd.*)

Item	*Tractor Operated Farms*				
	Marginal	*Small*	*Semi-medium*	*Medium*	*Large*
No. of farms surveyed	10	4	2	1	Nil
Total area operated (in ha)	6.12	3.32	3.22	2.43	
Average area per operated farm (in ha)	0.61	0.83	1.66	2.43	
Total crop production (in kg)	16,720	7,320	7,400	6,000	Nil
Average production per operated farm (in kg)	1,672	1,830	3,700	6,000	
A. Energy consumption per operated farm (in HP)					
I. Pre-harvest operations					
1. Tilling of land	86.05	118.09	331.07	214.80	
2. Sowing of seed	13.47	23.42	36.85	53.94	
3. Seed consumed	427.29	537.06	1225.25	1619.28	
4. Weeding	1.09	2.04	4.09	—	
5. Watering	27.54	7.91	57.39	268.50	
6. Fertilizer	3471.64	3435.85	6871.92	13408.20	
Sub-total	4027.10	4119.39	8526.61	15564.73	Nil
II. Post-harvest operations					
1. Harvesting	2.24	3.07	6.14	9.00	
2. Drying of produce	2.99	4.09	8.19	11.99	
3. Threshing	185.59	203.13	410.17	666.00	
Sub-total	190.83	210.30	425.04	686.99	Nil
Grand Total (I + II)	4217.93	4329.69	8951.65	16251.73	Nil
B. Crop Production (in HP)	9012.08	9863.70	19943.00	32340.00	
C. Energy Consumption (in HP)	4217.93	4329.69	8951.65	16251.73	
Energy Efficiency Index	2.13	2.27	2.22	1.98	

Appendix-VIII (*Contd.*)

Item	*Tractor-bullock Operated Farms*				
	Marginal	*Small*	*Semi-medium*	*Medium*	*Large*
No. of farms surveyed	1	1	1	Nil	Nil
Total area operated (in ha)	0.97	1.09	1.29		
Average area per operated farm (in ha)	0.97	1.09	1.29		
Total crop production (in kg)	3,800	2,000	4,480	Nil	Nil
Average production per operated farm (in kg)	3,800	2,000	4,480		
A. Energy consumption per operated farm (in HP)					
I. Pre-harvest operations					
1. Tilling of land	322.07	120.83	113.98		
2. Sowing of seed	0.77	0.87	1.03		
3. Seed consumed	647.71	831.23	863.61		
4. Weeding	—	5.40	3.18		
5. Watering	150.30	4.49	10.47		
6. Fertilizer	9385.74	4692.87	5368.28		
Sub-total	10506.59	5655.69	6355.55	Nil	Nil
II. Post-harvest operations					
1. Harvesting	3.59	4.05	4.77		
2. Drying of produce	4.79	5.40	6.36		
3. Threshing	532.80	222.00	497.28		
Sub-total	541.19	231.45	508.42	Nil	Nil
Grand Total (I + II)	11047.79	5887.14	6836.97	Nil	Nil
B. Crop Production (in HP)	20482.00	10780.0	24147.20		
C. Energy Consumption (in HP)	11047.79	5887.14	6863.97		
Energy Efficiency Index	1.85	1.83	3.51		

APPENDIX IX

A COMPARATIVE ANALYSIS OF ENERGY EFFICIENCY IN WHEAT PRODUCTION OF DIFFERENT FARMS IN SELECTED VILLAGES OF ATRAULI BLOCK OF ATRAULI TAHSIL IN ALIGARH DISTRICT

Item	*Bullock Operated Farms*				
	Marginal	*Small*	*Semi-medium*	*Medium*	*Large*
No. of farms surveyed	4	3	11	7	Nil
Total area operated (in ha)	1.70	2.09	12.70	16.33	
Average area per operated farm (in ha)	0.42	0.69	1.15	2.33	
Total crop production (in kg)	5,600	7,200	40,220	45,400	Nil
Average production per operated farm (in kg)	1,400	2,400	3,656	6,485	
A. Energy consumption per operated farm (in HP)					
I. Pre-harvest operations					
1. Tilling of land	3.98	4.06	8.32	19.34	
2. Sowing of seed	0.86	0.90	1.50	3.04	
3. Seed consumed	445.30	489.38	794.45	1557.39	
4. Weeding	0.84	0.92	0.32	1.86	
5. Watering	14.47	4.97	60.19	23.59	
6. Fertilizer	4525.26	2905.11	4621.40	9671.63	
Sub-total	4990.74	3405.44	5486.20	11192.76	Nil
II. Post-harvest operations					
1. Harvesting	2.47	2.57	4.27	8.64	
2. Drying of produce	3.29	3.43	5.69	11.52	
3. Threshing	155.40	266.40	405.85	732.67	
Sub-total	161.17	272.41	415.83	752.75	Nil
Grand Total (I + II)	5151.91	3677.86	5902.03	12031.23	Nil
B. Crop Production (in HP)	7546.00	12936.00	19705.84	34954.15	
C. Energy Consumption (in HP)	5151.91	3677.86	5902.03	12031.23	
Energy Efficiency Index	1.46	3.51	3.33	2.90	

Appendix-IX (*Contd.*)

Item	*Tractor Operated Farms*				
	Marginal	*Small*	*Semi-medium*	*Medium*	*Large*
No. of farms surveyed	Nil	1	6	4	Nil
Total area operated (in ha)		1.21	9.06	6.71	
Average area per operated farm (in ha)		1.21	1.51	1.67	
Total crop production (in kg)	Nil	3,800	25,440	20,360	Nil
Average production per operated farm (in kg)		3,800	4,240	5,090	
A. Energy consumption per operated farm (in HP)					
I. Pre-harvest operations					
1. Tilling of land		133.64	180.22	197.07	
2. Sowing of seed		26.85	35.53	37.26	
3. Seed consumed		809.640	1108.30	1271.13	
4. Weeding		—	1.03	1.55	
5. Watering		9.82	40.87	15.33	
6. Fertilizer		5028.07	6423.28	7821.45	
Sub-total	Nil	6008.03	7787.25	9343.89	Nil
II. Post-harvest operations					
1. Harvesting		4.47	5.59	6.21	
2. Drying of produce		5.97	7.45	8.28	
3. Threshing		532.80	470.64	564.99	
Sub-total	Nil	543.25	483.69	579.49	Nil
Grand Total (I + II)	Nil	6551.29	8270.94	9923.30	Nil
B. Crop Production (in HP)		20482.00	22853.60	27435.10	
C. Energy Consumption (in HP)		6551.29	8270.94	9923.30	
Energy Efficiency Index		3.12	2.76	2.76	

Appendix-IX (*Contd.*)

Item	*Tractor-bullock Operated Farms*				
	Marginal	*Small*	*Semi-medium*	*Medium*	*Large*
No. of farms surveyed	1	4	3	Nil	Nil
Total area operated (in ha)	0.81	4.59	4.54		
Average area per operated farm (in ha)	0.81	1.14	1.51		
Total crop production (in kg)	2,200	13,270	12,240	Nil	Nil
Average production per operated farm (in kg)	2,200	3,430	4,080		
A. Energy consumption per operated farm (in HP)					
I. Pre-harvest operations					
1. Tilling of land	107.35	110.80	143.29		
2. Sowing of seed	1.94	2.54	3.55		
3. Seed consumed	539.76	801.54	1007.55		
4. Weeding	1.99	—	—		
5. Watering	6.61	8.77	8.50		
6. Fertilizer	4469.40	5782.28	7002.06		
Sub-total	5127.70	6706.05	8165.01	Nil	Nil
II. Post-harvest operations					
1. Harvesting	2.99	4.25	5.60		
2. Drying of produce	3.99	5.67	7.46		
3. Threshing	355.20	380.73	423.30		
Sub-total	362.19	390.64	436.35	Nil	Nil
Grand Total (I + II)	5489.26	7096.70	8601.36	Nil	Nil
B. Crop Production (in HP)	11858.00	18487.07	21991.20		
C. Energy Consumption (in HP)	5489.26	7096.70	8601.36		
Energy Efficiency Index	2.16	2.60	2.55		

APPENDIX X

A COMPARATIVE ANALYSIS OF ENERGY EFFICIENCY IN WHEAT PRODUCTION OF DIFFERENT FARMS IN SELECTED VILLAGES OF KHAIR BLOCK OF KHAIR TAHSIL IN ALIGARH DISTRICT

Item	*Bullock Operated Farms*				
	Marginal	*Small*	*Semi-medium*	*Medium*	*Large*
No. of farms surveyed	2	6	14	7	Nil
Total area operated (in ha)	1.29	8..01	24.85	20.48	
Average area per operated farm (in ha)	0.64	1.33	1.78	2.92	
Total crop production (in kg)	3,200	21,060	60,760	49,080	
Average production per operated farm (in kg)	1,600	3,510	4,340	7,011	Nil
A. Energy consumption per operated farm (in HP)					
I. Pre-harvest operations					
1. Tilling of land	5.12	10.49	15.19	27.74	
2. Sowing of seed	0.84	1.73	2.31	3.80	
3. Seed consumed	469.59	908.59	1226.03	2160.58	
4. Weeding	0.69	1.46	2.06	4.36	
5. Watering	2.08	81.13	59.49	232.09	
6. Fertilizer	3072.71	6368.89	8285.95	11173.50	
Sub-total	3551.05	7372.33	9591.01	13599.08	Nil
II. Post-harvest operations					
1. Harvesting	2.39	4.94	6.57	10.83	
2. Drying of produce	3.19	6.59	8.74	14.44	
3. Threshing	244.20	389.61	433.88	778.26	
Sub-total	249.79	401.15	449.20	803.55	Nil
Grand Total (I + II)	3800.85	7773.48	10025.93	14402.64	Nil
B. Crop Production (in HP)	8624.00	18918.90	23392.60	37789.29	
C. Energy Consumption (in HP)	3800.85	7773.48	10025.93	14402.64	
Energy Efficiency Index	2.26	2.43	2.33	2.62	

Appendix-X (*Contd.*)

Item	*Tractor Operated Farms*				
	Marginal	*Small*	*Semi-medium*	*Medium*	*Large*
No. of farms surveyed	4	9	6	3	1
Total area operated (in ha)	1.21	8.71	12.22	12.55	4.86
Average area per operated farm (in ha)	0.30	0.96	0.03	4.18	4.86
Total crop production (in kg)	3,400	20,640	25,440	33,000	12,000
Average production per operated farm (in kg)	860	2,293	4,240	11,000	12,000
A. Energy consumption per operated farm (in HP)					
I. Pre-harvest operations					
1. Tilling of land	51.44	156.44	288.82	1267.09	751.81
2. Sowing of seed	6.74	21.69	45.21	92.83	107.88
3. Seed consumed	283.37	728.07	1650.76	2788.76	3238.56
4. Weeding	0.69	0.77	—	3.33	23.99
5. Watering	26.78	46.47	24.72	124.60	751.81
6. Fertilizer	2597.83	3823.82	7746.96	19533.62	26816.60
Sub-total	2966.87	4787.79	9756.48	23830.24	31690.45
II. Post-harvest operations					
1. Harvesting	1.12	3.58	7.54	15.88	17.99
2. Drying of produce	1.49	4.78	10.05	20.65	23.99
3. Threshing	95.46	254.56	433.64	1221.00	1332.00
Sub-total	98.08	262.92	451.24	1257.13	1373.98
Grand Total (I + II)	3064.96	5037.38	10207.73	25087.38	33064.43
B. Crop Production (in HP)	4635.40	12359.27	22853.60	59290.00	64680.00
C. Energy Consumption (in HP)	3064.96	5037.38	10207.73	25087.38	33064.43
Energy Efficiency Index	1.51	2.45	2.23	2.36	1.95

Appendix-X (*Contd.*)

Item	*Tractor-bullock Operated Farms*				
	Marginal	*Small*	*Semi-medium*	*Medium*	*Large*
No. of farms surveyed	3	4	5	5	Nil
Total area operated (in ha)	2.18	4.45	5.09	8.12	
Average area per operated farm (in ha)	0.75	1.11	1.01	1.62	
Total crop production (in kg)	5,100	11,000	13,320	37,400	Nil
Average production per operated farm (in kg)	1,700	2,750	2,664	7,480	
A. Energy consumption per operated farm (in HP)					
I. Pre-harvest operations					
1. Tilling of land	78.69	113.62	125.07	339.98	
2. Sowing of seed	1.74	0.11	2.26	1,300	
3. Seed consumed	518.16	782.65	701.68	1123.60	
4. Weeding	0.79	1.67	0.79	2.79	
5. Watering	30.16	7.01	5.70	434.18	
6. Fertilizer	3352.05	5167.74	5296.23	9383.56	
Sub-total	3981.62	6072.81	5131.74	11285.41	Nil
II. Post-harvest operations					
1. Harvesting	2.69	4.12	3.77	6.35	
2. Drying of produce	3.59	5.49	5.02	8.47	
3. Threshing	207.20	307.75	237.50	830.28	
Sub-total	213.49	314.87	701.04	845.11	Nil
Grand Total (I + II)	4195.12	6387.68	6832.80	12130.52	Nil
B. Crop Production (in HP)	9163.00	14822.50	14358.96	40317.20	
C. Energy Consumption (in HP)	4195.12	6387.68	6832.80	12130.52	
Energy Efficiency Index	2.18	2.32	2.10	3.32	

APPENDIX XI

A COMPARATIVE ANALYSIS OF ENERGY EFFICIENCY IN WHEAT PRODUCTION OF DIFFERENT FARMS IN SELECTED VILLAGES OF AKRABAD BLOCK OF AKRABAD TAHSIL IN ALIGARH DISTRICT

Item	*Bullock Operated Farms*				
	Marginal	*Small*	*Semi-medium*	*Medium*	*Large*
No. of farms surveyed	10	22	19	2	Nil
Total area operated (in ha)	5.95	18.91	26.14	8.91	
Average area per operated farm (in ha)	0.59	0.85	1.37	4.45	
Total crop production (in kg)	14,460	60,350	77,320	33,000	
Average production per operated farm (in kg)	1,446	2,743	4,069	16,500	
A. Energy consumption per operated farm (in HP)					
I. Pre-harvest operations					
1. Tilling of land	4.02	5.40	9.60	24.51	
2. Sowing of seed	0.77	1.10	1.80	5.79	
3. Seed consumed	441.87	641.83	1053.14	22481.00	
4. Weeding	1.46	0.30	0.52	—	
5. Watering	34.25	36.67	54.88	29.25	
6. Fertilizer	2860.41	4027.53	5498.59	18436.27	
Sub-total	3342.80	4712.85	6618.01	40977.52	Nil
II. Post-harvest operations					
1. Harvesting	2.20	3.18	5.13	16.49	
2. Drying of produce	2.93	4.24	6.17	21.99	
3. Threshing	160.50	304.46	412.21	1831.50	
Sub-total	165.64	311.90	423.51	1869.98	Nil
Grand Total (I + II)	3508.45	5024.75	7041.53	42847.50	Nil
B. Crop Production (in HP)	7793.94	14784.77	21931.91	88935.00	
C. Energy Consumption (in HP)	3508.45	5024.75	7041.53	42847.50	
Energy Efficiency Index	2.22	2.94	3.11	2.07	

Appendix-XI (*Contd.*)

Item	*Tractor Operated Farms*				
	Marginal	*Small*	*Semi-medium*	*Medium*	*Large*
No. of farms surveyed	16	9	6	6	5
Total area operated (in ha)	6.74	5.41	8.32	16.88	18.11
Average area per operated farm (in ha)	0.42	0.77	1.38	2.81	3.62
Total crop production (in kg)	16,480	15,040	19,000	50,100	69,020
Average production per operated farm (in kg)	1,030	2,148	3,166	8,350	13,804
A. Energy consumption per operated farm (in HP)					
I. Pre-harvest operations					
1. Tilling of land	51.87	98.68	145.03	456.09	244.95
2. Sowing of seed	8.80	17.15	30.79	62.32	80.39
3. Seed consumed	305.37	512.12	724.01	1988.11	2590.85
4. Weeding	0.54	0.59	1.29	3.36	1.34
5. Watering	28.78	19.34	110.72	67.49	114.43
6. Fertilizer	2419.76	3080.69	4774.76	13220.10	11329.97
Sub-total	2815.15	3728.60	5786.63	15464.17	14361.93
II. Post-harvest operations					
1. Harvesting	1.65	2.86	5.13	10.39	13.41
2. Drying of produce	2.08	3.81	6.85	13.86	17.88
3. Threshing	114.33	238.49	412.50	926.75	1532.24
Sub-total	118.06	245.16	424.48	951.01	1563.53
Grand Total (I + II)	2933.21	3973.34	6211.11	16415.18	15925.46
B. Crop Production (in HP)	5551.70	11577.72	17064.74	45006.50	74403.56
C. Energy Consumption (in HP)	2933.21	3973.34	6211.11	16415.18	15925.46
Energy Efficiency Index	1.89	2.91	2.74	2.74	4.67

Appendix-XI (*Contd.*)

Item	*Tractor-bullock Operated Farms*				
	Marginal	*Small*	*Semi-medium*	*Medium*	*Large*
No. of farms surveyed	1	4	3	Nil	Nil
Total area operated (in ha)	0.81	4.59	4.54		
Average area per operated farm (in ha)	0.81	1.15	1.51		
Total crop production (in kg)	1,900	13,720	12,240	Nil	Nil
Average production per operated farm (in kg)	1,900	3,430	4,080		
A. Energy consumption per operated farm (in HP)					
I. Pre-harvest operations					
1. Tilling of land	107.35	110.80	143.29		
2. Sowing of seed	0.64	0.92	1.21		
3. Seed consumed	539.76	801.54	1007.55		
4. Weeding	1.99	—	—		
5. Watering	6.61	8.77	8.50		
6. Fertilizer	4469.40	5782.28	7002.06		
Sub-total	5125.75	6704.31	8162.61	Nil	Nil
II. Post-harvest operations					
1. Harvesting	2.99	4.25	5.60		
2. Drying of produce	3.99	5.67	7.46		
3. Threshing	355.20	380.73	423.30		
Sub-total	362.19	390.64	436.35	Nil	Nil
Grand Total (I + II)	5487.95	7094.95	8598.96	Nil	Nil
B. Crop Production (in HP)	10241.00	18487.70	21991.20		
C. Energy Consumption (in HP)	5487.95	7094.95	8598.96		
Energy Efficiency Index	1.86	2.60	2.55		

Bibliography

Allen, B. and Hamilton Inc., *Energy Use in the Food System*, Federal Energy Administration, Washington, D.C., 1976.

Bansal, N.K. *et al.*, Effect of Improved Implements on the Pattern of Energy Utilization in Agriculture, *Agriculture, Ecosystems and Environment*, Vol. 25, No. 1, Jan. 1989, pp. 1-9.

Berardi, G.M., Organic and Conventional Wheat Production : Examination of Energy and Economics, *Agro-Ecosystems*, Vol. 4, 1978, pp. 367-76.

Biswas, A.K. and Biswas, M.R., Energy and Food Production, *Agro-Ecosystems*, Vol. 12, 1975, pp. 195-210.

Blight, G.L. *et al.* Trends in Energy, Usage, Energy Food Conversion and Relative Energy Efficiency of Primary Food Crops in Selected Countries, *Indian Journal of Agricultural Science*, Vol. 52, No. 7, 1982, pp. 417-23.

Borgstrom, G., Food, Feed and Energy, *Ambio*, Vol. 2, 1973, pp. 214-19.

Briggle, L.D., Introduction to Energy Use in Wheat Production. In : *Handbook of Energy Utilization Agriculture* (ed. D. Pimental), CRC Press, Bola Raton, Florida, 1980, pp. 109-16.

Brown, W.A.N. and R.G. Pearson, The Energy Requirements of Farming in New Zealand, Agricultural Economics Research Unit, *Research Report No. 80*, Lincoln College, Conterbury, New Zealand, 1977.

Cervinka, V.W.J. *et al.*, *Energy Requirements for Agriculture in California*, California Department of Food and Agriculture, Sacramento and Agricultural Engineering Department, University of California, Davis, January 1974.

Chancellor, W.J., The Role of Fuel and Electrical Energy in Increasing Production from Tradition Based Agriculture, *Transactions of the American Society of Agricultural Engineers (ASAE)*, Vol. 21, 1978, pp. 160-68.

Dekkers, W.A. *et al.*, Energy Production and Use in Dutch Agriculture, *Netherlands Journal of Agricultural Sciences*, Vol. 22, 1974, pp. 107-18.

Dazhong, W. and Pimental, D., Energy Use in Crop Systems in Northeastern China. In : *Food and Energy Resources* (eds. D. Pimental and C.W. Hall), New York, 1984.

Dvoskin, D. and Heady, E.O., Farming Practices Environmental Quality and the Energy Crisis, *Agriculture and Environment*, Vol. 3, 1976, pp. 1-13.

Fluck, R.C., Fundamentals of Energy Analysis for Agriculture. In: *Agricultural Energy*, Vol. 1, Solar Energy and Livestock Production, Proceedings of the ASAE National Energy Symposium, 29 Sept. - 1 Oct., Kansas City, MO. 1980, pp. 208-11.

F.A.O., Energy and Agriculture, *The State of Food and Agriculture 1976*, Rome, pp. 81-111.

Giriappa, S., *Energy Environment in Agriculture : A Study of Developed and Developing Systems*, New Delhi, Ashish, 1986.

Gupta, R.S.R. *et al.*, Energetics on Bullock - and Tractor-Powered Farms in India, *Energy in Agriculture*, Vol. 2, 1983, pp.153-60.

Gupta, R.S.R., Energy Utilization in Maize Production, *Energy*, Vol. 9, No. 2, Feb. 1984, pp. 189-92.

Giffard, R.M., Energy in Agriculture, *Search*, Vol. 7, 1976a, p. 411.

Gifford, R.M., and Millington, R.J., Energetics of Food Production with Special Emphasis on the Australian Situation, UNESCO, *Man and Biosphere Symposium : Energy and How We Live*, 1973.

Gupta, R.R. and Chaudhary, M.K., Level and Pattern of Energy Use and Working Cost of Post-harvest Operations of Wheat in Haryana, *Urja*, Vol. 13, Jan.-June 1983.

Heichel, G.H., Agricultural Production and Energy Resources, *American Scientist*, Vol. 64, 1976, pp. 64-72.

— —, Comparative Efficiency of Energy Use in Crop Production, *Bulletin 739*, Connecticut Agricultural Experiment Station, New Haven, 1973.

Hipsley, E.H., The Relationship Between Energy Utilization and Food Production - The Examples of New Guinea and Australia, *Food and Nutrition*, Vol. 24, 1967, pp. 6-13.

Hirst, E. Efficiency of Energy Use in the United States, *Science*, Vol. 1299, No. 6, 30 March 1973.

— —, *Energy Use for Food in the United States*, Oak Ridge National Laboratory, Environmental Programme, ORNL-NSF-EP-57, 1973.

Hudson, J.C., Sugarcane : Its Energy Relationships with Fossil Fuel, *Span*, Vol. 18, No. 12, 1975.

Jones, D.P., Energy Considerations in Crop Protection, *Outlook on Agriculture*, Vol. 8, No. 3, 1974, p. 141.

Jyothisri, M. and Singh, I., Optimization of Energy Inputs on Small Farms, *Urja*, Vol. 13, Jan.-June 1983, p. 231.

Kuether, D.O. and Duff, J.B., Energy Requirement for Alternative Rice Production Systems in the Tropics, IRRI, *Research Paper Series 59*, 1981.

Leach, G., Energy and Food Production, *Food Policy*, Vol. 1, 1975b, pp. 62-73.

— —, *Energy and Food Production*, International Institute for Environment and Development, London, 1975.

Lewis, D. and Tatchell, J., Energy in U.K. Agriculture, *J. Sci. Food Agric.*, Vol. 30, 1979, pp. 449-457.

Lockeretz, W. *et al.*, Organic and Conventional Crop Production in the Corn Belt : A Comparison of Economic Performance and Energy Use for Selected Farms, Centre for Biology of Natural Systems, Washington University, St. Louis, MO, 1976.

Lockeretz, W. (ed.) *Agriculture and Energy*, Academic Press, New York, 1977.

— —, Energy Inputs for Nitrogen, Phosphorus, and Potash Fertilizers. In : *Handbook of Energy Utilization in Agriculture*, CRC Press, Boca Raton, 1980.

Makhijani, A. and Poole, A., *Energy and Agriculture in the Third World*, Cambridge, Massachuesetts : Ballinger, 1975.

Pandey, V.K. *et al.*, Comparative Economics of Various Sources of Farm Energy in Haryana's Agriculture, *Urja*, Vol. 13, Jan.-June 1983.

Patterson, M.G., Energy Use in the New Zealand Food System, *Energy in Agriculture*, Vol. 3, No. 4, 1984, pp. 389-404.

Pearson, R.G. and Corbet, P.S., Energy in New Zealand Agriculture, *Search*, Vol. 7, 1976, pp. 418-23.

Pimental, D., Food Production and the Energy Crisis, *Science*, Vol. 182, 1973, pp. 443-49.

— —, The Energy Crisis : Its Impact on Agriculture. In : *Encyclopedia deno Scienza e della Technica*, Annuario delca EST, Mondadori, Milan, 1976, pp. 251-66.

Pimental, D. and Beyer, N., *Energy in Indian Agriculture*, Brookhaven National Laboratory and Cornell University, Ithaca, NY, draft, 1976.

Pimental, D. and Burgess, M., Energy Inputs in Corn Production. In : *Handbook of Energy Utilization in Agriculture*, CRC Press, Boca Raton, 1980, pp. 67-84.

Pimental, D. and Pimental, M., *Food, Energy and Society*, London, 1979.

——, Energy Flows in Agricultural and Natural Ecosystems. Options Mediterraneans, CIHEAMIAMZ-84-1, 1984, pp. 135-36.

Price, J.D., Energy Considerations in Crop Production, *Outlook on Agriculture*, Vol. 8, 1975, p. 141.

Ruttan, V.W., Food Production and the Energy Crisis : A Comment, *Science*, Vol. 187, 14 Feb. 1975, pp. 560-61.

Schipper, L., Raising the Productivity of Energy Utilization, *Annual Review of Energy*, Vol. 1, 1976, pp. 455-518.

Sehara, D.B.S. and Purohit, M.L., An Economic Analysis of Energy Utilization for Major Crops in Different Farming Systems in the Villages of Western Rajasthan, *Annals of Arid Zone*, Vol. 21, No. 4, 1982, pp. 219-23.

Sinha, S.K., Energy Balance in Agriculture : The Developing World. In: *Global Aspects of Food Production* (eds. M.S. Swaminathan and S.K. Sinha), Tycooly, Oxford, 1986, pp. 57-83.

Singh, G. and Chancellor, W., Energy Inputs and Agricultural Production Under Various Regimes of Mechanization in North India, *Transactions of the ASAE*, Vol. 18, 1975, pp. 252-59.

Smil, V. Nachman, P. and Long, T. II., *Energy Analysis and Agriculture: An Application to U.S. Corn Production*, West View, Boulder, CO, 1983.

Shafi, M., Farm Power and Productivity in Indian Agriculture, *Annals of the NAGI*, Vol. 5, No. 2, Dec. 1985, pp. 10-15.

Sharma, R. and Moorti, T.V., Human and Bullock Energy Consumption of Different Sizes of Farms in Paonta Valley of Himachal Pradesh, *Journal of the Society of Agricultural Statistics*, Vol. 29, No. 1, 1977, pp. 133-34.

Slesser, M., Energy Requirements of Agriculture. In : *Food, Agriculture and Environment* (eds. J. Leninhan and W.W. Fletcher), Glasgow : Blackie, 1975, pp. 1-20.

Stanhill, G. Energy and Agriculture : A National Case Study, *Agro-Ecosystems*, Vol. 1, No. 205, 1974, pp. 205-17.

Steinhart, J.S. and Steinhart, C.E., Energy Use in the United States Food System. In : *Perspective on Energy* (eds. Lon C. Ruedisile and M.W. Firebaugh), New York, 1978, pp. 46-61.

Turhune, E.C., Prospects for Increasing Food Production in LDCs through Efficient Energy Utilization. In : *Agriculture and Energy* (ed. W. Lockeretz), New York, 1977, pp. 625-38.

Walker, L.P. *et al.*, Method for Modelling and Evaluating Integrated Energy Systems in Agriculture, *Energy in Agriculture*, Vol. 3, No. 1, May 1984, pp. 1-27.

White, D.J., Efficient Use of Energy in Agriculture, *The Agricultural Engineer*, Vol. 34, No. 3, 1979, pp. 67-70.

— —, Agriculture and Energy, *Agricultural Progress*, Vol. 50, 1975, p. 39.

— —, The Use of Energy in Agriculture, *Farm Management*, Vol. 2, No. 12, Summer 1975, p. 637.

— —, Energy in Agricultural Systems, Conference on the Use of Energy in Agriculture, Institute of Agricultural Engineers, 13 May 1975, *The Agricultural Engineer*, Vol. 30, No. 3, Autumn, 1975.

Watt, M., An Energy Analysis of the Australian Food System, *Energy in Agriculture*, Vol. 3, No. 4, 1984, pp. 279-88.

Index